MASS VIOLENCE IN AMERICA

MASS VIOLENCE IN AMERICA

A REVIEW OF THE CATTLE BUSINESS IN JOHNSON COUNTY, WYOMING SINCE 1892 AND THE CAUSES THAT LED TO THE RECENT INVASION

Oscar H. Flagg

ARNO PRESS & THE NEW YORK TIMES

New York • 1969

*

Library of Congress Catalog Card No. 79–90174

*

Manufactured in the United States of America

*

This work was originally published in 1892 as a series of articles in the *Buffalo* (Wyoming) *Bulletin*.

*

The Publisher wishes to express its gratitude to the Wyoming State Archives and Historical Department for providing the copy used in the preparation of this edition.

Editorial Note

NATIONS, LIKE MEN, ARE SOMETIMES INTERESTED IN BURYING THE PAST.

In early 1968, after more than five years marked by political assassinations, racial uprisings, campus disorders, mass demonstrations and the violent suppression of protest, *The New York Times Magazine* asked a group of distinguished scholars to reply to the question, "Is America by nature a violent society?" In answer, University of Chicago anthropologist Clifford Geertz wrote:

> "We do not know very well what kind of society we live in, what kind of history we have had, what kind of people we are. We are just now beginning to find out, the hard way . . ."

The proposition was astonishing but correct: what was least understood about domestic political violence was its role in American history. It was common knowledge that the United States had had a Revolution, a Civil War, some trouble with the Indians and a period of labor-management conflict. But one could search the shelves of the nation's great libraries without discovering more than a handful of works on the subject of violence in American history, and these hopelessly out of date.

Historians had generally ignored or soft-pedaled the history of farmer uprisings, native vigilantism, labor-management struggles, ethnic conflicts and race riots; comparative work in the history of social conflict was particularly weak. Sociologists and political scientists in the grip of "consensus" theory tended to treat episodes of mass violence in America as insignificant or aberrational—temporary exceptions to the norm of peaceful progress. Psychologists and behavioral scientists discussed "mob violence" in terms which suggested that riots, revolts, insurrections and official violence were the products of individual or group pathology. All such interpretations had the effect not only of minimizing group violence in America, but of depriving it of political content—hence, of relevance to the present.

As a result, as late as 1968, the rich, multifarious and often terrifying history of domestic political violence was still largely *terra incognita*. So long as most Americans wished to keep certain skeletons locked away in their closets, few scholars would attempt to open doors. Conversely, once the American people, frightened yet emboldened by the sudden reappearance of intense social conflict, began to ask new questions about the past, so did the scholars.

Our purpose in helping Arno Press and *The New York Times* select and publish significant documents in the history of political violence has not been to compound past errors by overemphasizing the role of conflict in American history. On the contrary, our aim has been to provide materials which will aid in the search for an accurate perspective on the present. MASS VIOLENCE IN AMERICA includes eyewitness reports, government documents and other descriptive and analytic material relating to mass political violence in the United States. These documents not only provide information—they give the "feel" or "flavor" of past eras of civil disorder by evoking the emotional and political context in which revolts took place. Most of them have long been out of print and are obtainable, if at all, only in the nation's largest libraries.

The scope of this series is wide, ranging from accounts of Indian warfare to descriptions of labor-management violence, from narratives of colonial insurrections to reports on modern racial uprisings. It is not, however, limitless, nor were the constituent volumes carelessly selected. The principle of coherence which guided the selections is implicit in the phrase "mass political violence." "Mass" denotes activity engaged in by large groups rather than individuals acting alone; "political" suggests a relationship between such activity and competition among domestic groups for power, property and prestige; and "violence" is narrowly construed as resulting in physical damage to persons or property. In short, the materials reproduced herein are intended to illuminate the resort to violence by American groups seeking to change or to preserve the status quo. Although historical, they are of interest to any who wishes to understand the causes, nature and direction of domestic political violence, whether they be social scientists, historians or just interested Americans.

Of course, we are particularly hopeful that these volumes will prove useful to those now engaged in curriculum-revision and the teaching of high school and college courses in the area of American studies. What Christopher Jencks and David Reisman term "the Academic Revolution" has made difficult demands on all educators, not the least of which is the demand for courses which are both relevant to the condition of modern America and of the highest academic quality. These volumes are meant to provide raw material for such courses—primary source matter which will help both instructors and students to deepen and enrich their views of the American experience.

Most important, the editors and publisher recognize that these volumes appear during a national crisis which is also a crisis of the spirit, a time in which the public response to various manifestations of civil disorder is increasingly governed by anger, fear and hysteria. In such an atmosphere it is important to recognize that one is not alone in time—that such events have taken place before in America and, unless fundamental changes in our social and political life take place, will probably recur in the future. Our fondest hope is that this work, and others like it, will help to keep alive, in a time of growing unreason, the spirit of reasoned inquiry.

RICHARD E. RUBENSTEIN
The Adlai Stevenson Institute
Chicago, Illinois

ROBERT M. FOGELSON
Harvard-MIT Joint Center for Urban Studies
Cambridge, Massachusetts

PUBLISHER'S NOTE

In 1820 O. H. Flagg, editor of the *Buffalo* (Wyoming) *Bulletin* wrote a series of articles giving a first-hand account of the role of the large cattle interests in Johnson County, Wyoming. Because they offer a vivid example of the bloody range wars of the time, these articles are included in MASS VIOLENCE IN AMERICA.

A REVIEW OF
THE CATTLE BUSINESS IN
JOHNSON COUNTY, WYOMING

A REVIEW OF THE CATTLE BUSINESS IN JOHNSON COUNTY, WYOMING, SINCE 1892, AND THE CAUSES THAT LED TO THE RECENT INVASION

The writer came to Johnson county in the fall of 1882, with a herd of cattle from Texas, and since then has been a continuous resident.

The state of Wyoming has for years been considered as furnishing the best natural feeding grounds for cattle of any of the western states, and that fact has been taken advantage of by Americans, Englishmen and Frenchmen. Fortunes have been invested in stock, and in cases where the herds have been managed judiciously, handsome profits have been realized, whereas, on the contrary, as I will show, great loss has followed.

In the year 1882 the stock business was at a height of prosperity, seldom equalled by any business; men flushed with success, sent the glad news flying over the world, and soon capitalists were crowding each other in their efforts to buy the golden cow.

The rich succulent grass grew high over the hills and valley, the flush mountain streams afforded a bountiful supply of water; buffalo elk and deer roamed the grasses along the foothills of the snowcapped mountains, affording both food and sport for the easterner and Englishman, and the crack of the sportsmens rifle could be heard echoing in the mountain, as he wantonly slayed the game.

Herd after herd was driven into the county, fabulous prices were paid for cattle, in fact, some owners had cattle that cost them $60 per head. Beef steers would realize their owners $75 to $80 per pound, everything was prosperous, and everybody joyful.

Hundreds of men were in the county working as cowboys; men were in demand all the time to handle the big herds; money was no object, and big wages were paid, which were spent at the earliest opportunity. The majority of the cattle in this county at this time, were owned by Englishmen, who carried everything on a grand scale.

They built fine ranch houses at great expense, fitted them out with furniture from the old country, including pianos, etc. laid in stocks of wines and whiskies, had valets to attend to their every want, brought their families out in the summer to enjoy the bracing air of the mountains, and to recuperate their energies, wasted in the crowded cities during the preceding winter.

The spring roundup of 1883 was one long to be remembered by the boys who took a hand in that great drive. On the 20th of May, twenty-seven wagons, with a full complement of men and horses met at the mouth of Crazy Woman.

Fred Hesse, was the foreman of the whole outfit. On that occasion about 1,400 head of horses, and 400 men were present; the sight was a beautiful one. For two miles along the river the wagons were camped, in order to afford room for the different bunches of horses to graze without becoming mixed.

About sunrise on the morning of the 21st the men all collected at a certain place designated by the foreman preparatory to starting on the different drives. This was the first day of the round-up, every man rode his best horse, and each one vied with the other in the splendor of his rig.

Shouts of laughter could be heard now and then, as some tenderfoot would be thrown from his bucking horse, and such exclamations as "stay with him!" "Jump off!" "Spur him in the eye!" would be yelled at some other poor fellow who would be striving with tooth and toe nail to stick on his unmanagable steed.

All collected, the foreman would say to the man, "you take forty men and drive such and such a place," to another he would say, "you take fifty men and drive such and such a place," and so on until all of the men were sent out on the respective drives.

About 9 o'clock the drivers would begin to get in; one drive would bring in 1,000 head, another 1,500 head, and so on until something like 7,000 head were driven together. They were separated into four different bunches, and then the different outfits would begin to get out their cows and calves.

By 3 o'clock work was over, and the boys with the exception of the few who were left on herd, were free to do as they chose. Card playing, horse racing, foot racing, etc., were then in order for the rest of the day, and half the night.

Everyone had plenty of money. I remember seeing a party of fifteen boys spinning a top, each one putting in $1, the winner taking $14.

The second day was a petition of the first, and so on for months, until all of the country had been worked over. Thousands of calves were branded, and train after train steamed into Chicago that fall loaded with fat beef, which brought top prices.

The Cattle Baron's heart was light, and his pocketbook heavy with money made off the free ranges of Wyoming. The Englishmen rejoicing over their good luck, made haste to get back to the old country with the wealth they had acquired through the generosity of Uncle Sam.

The Maverick Question in 1883

In 1883 there was no law regulating the maverick question. The country was divided into ranges, the boundary lines of which were defined by certain creeks and rivers, and the outfit claiming a range built corrals on it, and all the mavericks caught within its prescribed lines were branded with its brand.

More mavericks were branded that year than before or since; there was little confusion, and as the boundary lines were plain, few contentions arose.

There was, though, a strip of country lying on the head of Salt creek that was far distant from any ranch, and had never been thoroughly worked. It had been considered natural ground, and whoever got a maverick there, put his brand on it.

That spring the Powder River and Platte River round-ups both met there. Fred Hesse claimed the mavericks for the 76 outfit, and Searights' foreman claimed them for him. Something like 400 mavericks were caught in that strip. After a great deal of contention and bluffing, by both outfits, the matter was compromised, and each outfit took a share.

Now I want to show where to show where the honest baron's greed and dishonesty began to assert itself. They had given their words of honor that they would be honest and fair respecting the range and maverick question, and that a man who would take a maverick from another's range, had committed a theft.

Did they respect the promise given a gentlemen of honor? No! There were no small men then for them to steal from each other.

They did this, as boys still in the country can prove. An outfit would pay a man in its employ from $2 to $5 for every maverick he could rustle from a neighboring outfit. The writer made some money that way himself.

The country was owned--I might say--at that time, exclusively by the barons. With the exception of Jim Dowlin and J. R. Smith, there was not a small rancher between the Platte and Buffalo, or between Wind River and Little Missouri. The country was one vast feeding ground, over which their cattle grazed unrestricted.

No wire fences intercepted their course from one stream to another, and the odious settler of today never entered their golden dreams. They reigned supreme, no obstacle, with their money and influence, was too great for them to surmount.

They were foolish enough to think they could arrest in its course the march of progress and civilization.

They said, "Wyoming is ours, we will brook no interference from the man who wants to plow and till the soil, and build for himself a home in the midst of our ranges; the beautiful valleys and grassclad slopes are ours by right of discovery.

The bleat of our calves is sweeter to our ears, and the right of these fertile valleys, unpopulated and covered with our cattle, is pleasanter to our ears, then would be the prattle of the settler's children, and the right of comforable homes nestling among the hills, and surrounded by fields of waving grain. A beef steer is of greater consideration to us than a settler's comfort, or even his life."

I have shown that the year 1883 was a prosperous one for the barons. They had no cause for complaint, that year at least.

When fall work was over the majority of the boys employed during the summer were discharged. But they were welcome to stay at the different ranches until work opened the next spring. They would move about from one ranch to another, not often staying more than two weeks at the same place.

Amusements were generally free, but taking it all together, they enjoyed themselves very well, playing cribbage, etc.

The winter of 1883 and 1884 was a pretty hard one. The loss was considerable, but there were so many cattle in the country at the time that no estimate of the true loss could be arrived at.

About the first of May, 1884, the barons held their annual stock meeting in Cheyenne to arrange the different round-ups, and to try and solve the still important maverick riddle, that was the bone of contention, over which they were still snarling and wrangling.

Those of them who were inclined to be honest had cause for complaint at the way in which their dishonest compatriots had been encroaching upon their range rights.

The question was settled for the coming year in the following manner: the mavericks were to be gathered and held, and sold to the highest bidder from day to day, with the understanding that each man was to have the option on his range of buying them in at $10 per head.

The foreman of the round-up was auctioneer, with full authority to receive this money and receipt for same; he was required to give bonds to the association for the faithful performance of his duty.

The cowboys thought that so long as the mavericks were to be sold to the highest bidder that they here had a chance to buy cattle, but they were sadly mistaken. A bunch of mavericks would be put up for sale, some boy who had a few dollars saved up would make a bid on them, the baron who claimed the range, or his foreman who was acting for him, would then raise the bid, they would be run up so high that the cowboy would have to quit.

No matter how high the bid had been, the baron would be receipted for so many mavericks at $10 per head.

It was impossible for an employee to buy a cow.

The roundup started out in the spring of 1884 under very favorable auspices. Grass was plentiful, horses and cattle were fat, and the boys, chafing under the restrictions of the indoor life of the preceding winter were anxious to again be in the saddle, astride of their wiry ponies, to race over the boundless prairies, to inhale the pure air wafted from the Rockies, and laden with the perfume of spring flowers.

The gathering was a joyful one, friend greeted friend. Hand shakes were exchanged between boys who had been separated during the past winter.

Some of these boys having spent the winter in their homes in the east and in the adjoining states.

Some of the "barons" were there also. Englishmen in knee breeches, accompanied by their general managers, buggy bosses and valets, rode around with an air of lordliness which was ridiculous.

The following outfits with their respective foremen were there. The 76, F. G. S. Hesse; Bar C, H. W. Devoe; EK, Jack Donahue; N. H., Phil DuFran; LX Bar, Simon White; Hoe, Frank Labertaux; 21, Charley Morgareidge. Outside outfits had representatives. C. C. S. Ford and Nate Champion were both there.

Friends they were then, and poor Nate little dreamed at that time that the hand that grasped his then in friendship would some day be turned against him and would handle the gun that was to send a bullet through his heart.

The calf crop that spring was large and encouraging. The "barons" were still ready to buy cattle whenever offered for sale. The 76 brought in that summer several thousand head, for which they paid $40 a round, and the manager, Morton Frewen, claimed for the company 4,000 head; Hoe, 8,000; 21, 10,000; LX Bar, 20,000; Flying E, as many as 150,000 head of cattle ranging in Johnson county alone, not including the basin, which would probably raise the total to 200,000.

These figures will give one some idea of the enormity of the cattle business at that time. At the meeting of the directors of the 76 outfit held in London the fall of 1883 a divident of 35 percent was declared. Is it any wonder that men should want to invest their money in a business that would pay such a per cent on the money invested as that?

The 76 company claimed at that time as their range a scope of country comprising at least 75 miles square bounded on the south by Salt creek and South Powder which included the best grazing ground in the country.

In the spring of 1884 a man named J. N. Tisdale came right into the center of the range claimed by them and took 160 acres of government land. He was at the time supposed to be a poor man, and was treated with great contempt by Fred Hesse, foreman of the 76.

He was told that he would have to leave, that he was an intruder, that he would be boycotted by the 76 and other outfits. He did not have his hay meadow fenced yet when the round-up got to his place and the herds were driven over and held on his meadows. Indignities of all kinds were heaped upon him by the 76 outfit.

He bought 700 head of cattle, paying $60 a round for them. He was told that his cattle would not be handled by the other outfits, that no man of his would be allowed to go with the wagons of the 76. He came to the wagon one day himself to try and make some amicable arrangement with Hesse by which his cattle could be handled.

He was insulted, and when he undertook to resent the insule, came near being brained by Hesse with a branding iron.

He then appealed to the Bar C outfit which was then in charge of H. W. Devoe. Working in that outfit at the time was Nate Champion, Al Allison and myself. Nate was in charge of the wagon on the range most of the time.

Although the owners of the Bar C were opposed to Tisdale, Devoe and the rest of us felt sorry for him, we thought he had been treated unjustly, and Nate Champion told me that as long as he was in charge of the wagon he would brand his calves for him, even if he lost his situation by doing so. And he did it. He was a true friend to Tisdale; helped him in the time of adversity, and was his well wisher in time of prosperity.

It soon became known, though, that Tisdale, instead of being a poor man, was manager for one of the wealthiest companies that ever invested money in Wyoming. As soon as this fact was established beyond a doubt, Hesse was the first man to apologize, and to offer to admit him to the fold of the barons.

The wealth of his company soon began to assert itself; thousands of acres of government land were fenced in by him, and the ranch stocked with blooded stock, both of horses and cattle. In 1890 he was elected state senator, and Nate Champion voted for him. He is another one of the men who required of Champion his heart's blood for favors done in the past.

Once more the barons, after settling up their business in the fall, returned to their homes to enjoy the proceeds of their beeves, fattened upon the free ranges of Uncle Sam. Once more the worn-out cow ponies were turned loose upon their winter range; and the boys having been laid off, scattered, some to their home in the east, where loving mothers and sisters were anxiously waiting to greet them, some to the neighboring towns, where they would soon spend their easily earned money.

Again, some boy would seek the nearest postoffice, and with the exception of a few dollars, would send his money to a mother or sister who was depending solely upon him for support. I have met in the last seventeen years some noble boys, who were classed in the category as the primitive, untutored cowboy from Mexico. Boys, whose forms, though clad in leather and buckskin, carried in their breasts, hearts as noble as those of any of the heroes who have figured in the history of our country.

Once more the winter is approaching with its snow and ice, and many a long dreary day will have to be passed by the boys who are housed up at the different ranches, nothing to do but play cards and talk, each day a repetition of the one passed.

As darkness settles in the valleys and the last ray of the setting sun is lingering on the mountain top, as tho' loth to withdraw its warmth and light from the snow bound earth, and Boreas, with his icy blast is roaring through the canyons and around the log houses, driving to shelter the poor brutes exposed to his merciless fury, a roaring fire is built in the huge fireplace.

The boys gather around, tell stories and recount incidents connected with their work of the past summer, and talk over the prospects for the coming one. One fellow tells of a certain top cutting horse in his string, of how he can ride into the round up and cut out steers without a bridle.

Another tells of how he rode the best rope horse in the outfit, and tells of how he roped and tied down a 1,500 pound steer all alone to prove his prowess. A friendly bout is had with the boxing gloves, and then all prepare to turn into their bunks and dream of bucking broncs and fighting cows.

The dreary winter of 1884 and 1885 passed away. A right hard winter it was; and the barons in their comfortable clubs enjoying their wine and cigars, were apprehensive that their losses might be large. They could not form much of an idea though until the round ups started to work.

April, 1885

April of 1885 found them again in Cheyenne, having met to hold their annual meeting to lay out round ups and discuss the best plans for working their herds to the best advantage. The program laid out for the coming summer, was the same as that of the past one; mavericks were to go to the highest bidder.

The boys were put to work the first of April. Some repairing old and building new corrals and hauling wood to them, to be used for branding fires, others cleaning off hay meadows and opening up irrigating ditches. A good many young horses had to be ridden and gentled for the coming work. Wire fences had to be built, and various jobs attended to, which kept everyone busy until the middle of May, the time designated for the round up to start.

After work had commenced the fears of the barons occasioned by the hard winter just passed, began to be realized.

There was a very perceptible falling off in the number of cattle that had in previous years been rounded up at the different rounding places. As each day still showed the same decrease, they would say, "the cattle drifted during the winter and we find them further to the south."

Day after day they worked south, but still the cattle failed to appear. Finally, after working over the entire range the barons had to submit to the inevitable and admit that their loss had been heavy.

The summer was hot and dry; there was scarcely any grass or water. As early as August stock were beginning to browse in the sagebrush and greasewood, and it was almost impossible to hold a bunch of round up horses on account of their wandering for grass and water.

The beeves gathered for market that fall were not fat, and the railroads carried to Chicago a very poor class of stock, which caused a big drop in prices. In previous years cattle brought from $5 to $6 per 100. That year they brought $2 and $3 per 100.

When work was over that year the books showed a very small calf tally, and after firing every man--only keeping one or two to look after the horses during the winter, the barons left with much lighter pocketbooks than formerly.

Some of the barons, encouraged by their success in former years, had made preparations for the ranch business on a grand and expensive scale.

They brought friends from the east and had them file on all the finest land, some of whom never saw the land again after it was filed upon. In fact, land was filed on in Johnson county at the Cheyenne land office by men who had never seen it. I know whereof I speak, because I am living on and have a patent for a piece of that land.

In some cases where 160 acres would be fenced in, and if a man looking for land would ask if the barons owned all the land fenced in, he would be told that they did. Large ditches were taken out of streams of water to this land, at a great expense. The Peters & Alston outfit, owned by foreigners, fenced in several thousand acres, not one foot of which was filed upon and prepared to ditch it. A large ditch, 12 feet on the bottom, was taken out by contract and the water turned in. The ditch ran over land composed of a gypsum foundation, which proved to be hollow, and after the water had run a short time, holes began to start in the ditch, which defied all efforts to stop them. Teams were kept busy hauling lumber a distance of sixty miles, with which to flume these holes, and $30 per 1,000 was paid for it. As fast as one hole was flumed another would start. After working on it for a year and spending $25,000, it was abandoned.

I cite this as an instance of their lack of judgment and management.

The Winter of 1885 and 1886

Passed, and April, 1886, once more found the barons congregated at Cheyenne. Some of them had evidently begun to lose a little of their faith in the country. Instead of being so eager to buy, they now wanted to sell, and during the winter some of them had induced parties who knew nothing of the condition of affairs to buy.

Many a young fellow has cause to regret that he ever met these oily tongued gentlemen, who, with their smooth talk made them think Wyoming was a paradise, and induced them to put their money into their stock companies.

The Peters & Alston Co. sold several thousand calves to two young fellows from Pennsylvania, and the O Bar O outfit sold several thousand head; the price paid being $13 per head. Several other outfits sold calves for the same price.

Although they were selling calves to these tenderfeet they would not sell a one to a cowboy or a poor man in the country.

The summer of 1886 was another dry one, and the calf crop was still smaller than that of the preceding summer. The price of beef was steadily on the decline, the range surely playing out, and the prospect looked very dark.

Expenses were curtailed in every way, the working force was curtailed in every way, the working force was cut down to one-half, and placards having the words in large letters, "Road Ranch, Meals 50 Cents" on them were put up in conspicuous places at nearly all of the ranches and boys out of employment were given to understand that they were not welcome to spend their winters at the cow ranches.

During the last two years a good many homesteads had been taken up by settlers, and some of the boys who had been working for the different outfits had filed on government land. Parties moving in from Nebraska and other states brought small bunches of stock with them; herds driving in from Texas would sell and trade lame and played out cattle, till finally a good many small bunches were owned by the settlers.

All these movements were looked upon as impositions by the "barons". They knew that a maverick was public property and that any man who owned cattle had a right to them. At the stock meeting in the spring of '86 wages were reduced from $40 to $35 per month, and as soon as the round-up started a strike was organized. All work was stopped and word sent to the different managers that no work would go on until they agreed to pay the former wages. They were caught at a disadvantage, work had to be shoved forward, they were obliged to brand their calves and gather beef, and as they had no time to get more men, were obliged to comply with the demands of the strikers and restore their wages. It was done under portest, and as soon as they could get men to fill their places the strikers were either fired or compelled to have their own wages reduced. That summer witnessed the last big round-up in Johnson county. It was not so large as those of former years, but much larger than any one held since.

The winter that was to prove the Waterloo of the barons was approaching.

The storms that were to sound their financial death knell and sweep from the plains of Wyoming the source of their wealth, were already gathering in the north. The grass, owing to the country having been overstocked for a number of years was entirely gone, and hardly a vestige of anything on which stock could subsist remained. By the middle of October winter had set in, and by the first of December the oldest settlers were declaring they had never seen anything to equal it. The whole country was nearly snow-bound. Freighters were compelled to stop on their way between Buffalo and the railroad and abandon their outfits, and in many cases their stock died from exposure.

The poor range cattle. What of them? They were getting weak by the first of November, and by December were already beginning to die. They were wandering over the country in droves; now and then on some hill where the wind had blown off the snow they would find, maybe, a mouthful of grass. They were crowded in all the river and creek bottoms eating off the willow, sagebrush and greasewood. Under banks, and in all protected places, the poor things crowded to get a little protection from the bitter wind, which chilled their poor emaciated forms to the bone and froze lots of them to death in their sheltered places. They were compelled to keep moving in order to keep from freezing, and their feet were cut by the frozen snow until their trail could be followed by the blood which flowed from them.

In January there was a thaw that lasted for a day or two, melting the snow and the whole country was covered with slush and water. This was followed immediately by severe cold which froze the water and then the country was a slippery glacier which proved to be a veritable death trap for the weakened cattle. Whenever the poor animals would slip and fall they were too weak to ever get upon their feet again. The loss was fearful; thousands of cattle perished; but the full extent of the loss could not be determined until the spring round-up started.

There was one baron, though, who could figure his loss pretty accurately, vis: J. N. Tisdale. He had two years before bought a herd of 700 cows, paying $60 a head for them. The bunch, already considerably depleted by the preceding hard winter, was brought in to his ranch where he intended to feed them hay. The winter was so long and severe that he ran out of hay, and nearly 400 of these $60 cows died around his stables and were dragged off, and he hardly saved the rest by hauling hay a distance of 35 miles, for which he had to pay $25 a ton.

The first green grass of 1887 was welcomed with joy by both man and beast; for six long, dreary months the poor cattle had wandered from place to place, hunting for warmth and food, and the great wonder was how any one of them had lived.

Once more the barons are found in Cheyenne to consider the cheapest way to find out what they had lost during the winter. The cattle trust was formed. Some of the smaller outfits, such as Games and some outfits let their cattle to other larger outfits to run at so much per head, thus cutting down the number of wagons generally put out. The EK Co. turned its cattle in to the trust to be tallied out that summer. In previous years so anxious had parties been to buy cattle that they did not require them tallied out, but would buy them from the books. The round-up that spring was a small affair; from 27 wagons the spring of 1883, the number had gradually been reduced until only four were present in 1887.

Round-up grounds, where in 1883 10,000 head of cattle had been rounded up, in 1887 only showed as many hundred. There was no fun, no excitement of any kind, the barons had instructed their foremen to allow no gambling around the wagons, no horse racing on company horses. The good old times were gone, and the boys were beginning to realize that they must take up land and establish homes for themselves or leave the country. Many of them had already taken up land, and many of the old timers had left the country. Such old timers as John Braziel, Twist Montgomery, T. Haines, Jim Baker, Ed Stewart, and scores of others had long since departed for "other fields and pastures green." At that time the barons all signed a paper, taken around by Horace Plunkett, agreeing to boycott all boys who had gone to ranching and had produce of any kind to sell. That spring I was black-balled and not allowed to work for any of the outfits because I had bought cattle and taken up government land.

At that time the duplicity of Fred Hesse showed itself. He was put in as manager by the EK to superintend the tallying of its herd to the trust. The way of tallying was to put EK on the shoulder of each and every animal. As fast as a bunch of 500 or 1,000 was gathered it was driven to the chute, and as each animal went through it was branded. The trust had a man also to see that they got a square deal. He was somewhat of a tenderfoot, and he either did not know or did not want to know what was going on. Work afterwards on the range developed the fact that hundreds of cattle not belonging to the EK had K on the shoulder, and also that the iron had been touched so lightly to lots of them that the brand would never peel. Hesse must have been paid pretty well for that work for it amounted to many thousands of dollars, dishonestly gained by the EK.

When work was over that fall the loss was estimated to have been 80 percent, and in some cases it was heavier. One man on the head of the Belle Fouche turned loose 2,500 head of through cattle the fall of 1886, and during 1887 he did not gather more than 100 head.

Another man declared his loss had been 120 percent. When asked how that could have been, he said, "I lost all that I had and it cost me 20 percent of what my herd was worth to find it out."

Mavericks were sold the summer of 1887 to the highest bidder as usual, but the crop was very small and very inferior, consisting mostly of what are called "poddies"--big bellied calves whose mothers had died in the spring.

Very few men were employed and there was very little romance connected with the summer's work. Ranger Jones (who was murdered by Canton last fall) came to Wyoming in the spring of 1887 and went to work for the EK outfit, which had for its foreman John Russell.

I could not work for any outfit on Powder River that spring; and as I had a string of horses of my own, and what few cattle I owned were ranging in the Cheyenne river and antelope country, I decided to go to that round-up.

J. B. Moore, now living in Sheridan, was foreman of the round-up. I worked for a few days with the 21 wagon and Moore offered to give me a job, which I was glad to accept. He was foreman at the time of the OC outfit which sold afterwards to the Ogallala company.

In conversation with Mr. Moore one day, I asked him if he would sell me mavericks, and much to my surprise he told me he would sell them to any man who had the money to pay for them. When the mavericks were sold the next day I was on hand and bought seven heifers, at $10 per head. My brand was put on them, and M (the association brand) was put on the neck of each one. I brought them home with me when I came in July.

The summer of 1887 was a little more favorable for the stock interests. There were very few cattle left in the country. One thing was certain though, what few were left were good, hardy young stock, and were not a bit crowded for range. The loss on Texas cattle and old cows was fully 90 percent, and as most of the outfits had a surplus of old cows on hand they all suffered. The loss on steer cattle was not so heavy, and the round-ups were rather devoid of cows and calves.

The EK continued to tally during the summer. Nothing of importance transpired in the cattle business. The barons were by this time beginning to feel pretty blue; they knew that the halycon days were gone, and that they would have to do some good scheming to get even on their losses.

The homesteader had been busy during this time. The fact had been thoroughly established that the soil of Wyoming was as fine as any in the United States, and would, when watered, produce splendid crops of anything planted. Vegetables of all kinds, as well as wheat and oats could not be excelled for both quality and quantity of yield in any country, and that fact had been taken advantage of.

On almost every creek large enough to furnish water for 160 acres of land could be found a rancher, with from one to fifty head of cattle. They did not have much of this world's goods, any of them, but their cabins were their castles, and they were as much "Lords of all they surveyed" as any one of the cattle barons; and little did they dream that in the near future they would be marked for death by these barons and their homes burned over their heads.

The weather continued good until late in the fall of 1887, and cattle went into the winter in good shape. There was no bad weather until after Christmas. The whole winter was an exceptionally good one.

There was a great change noticeable around the different ranches, where in former winters one could find from five to twenty boys at a ranch; at this time about four was the complement, and they found plenty of work to do.

Curt Spaugh came up from Rawhide Buttes and took charge of the EK outfit, and John Russell took the Bar C in place of H. W. Devoe, who had been foreman for several years.

The round-up met in the spring of 1888 on the north fork of Powder River on the 20th day of May. The outfits having wagons there were the 76, EK, and Pugsley, three wagons only. It commenced to rain the night of the 20th and rained continuously for ten days, stopping all work.

The rivers were all out of their banks and it was impossible to cross them. Ranger Jones, who had gone back to his home in Nebraska the previous when the work was over, came back and again went to work for the EK. He was a splendid rider and was a valuable man in an outfit. His greatest delight was in riding a pitching horse, and as the outfit had a great many of them, he had his hands full.

It was really wonderful to see him ride. He had such a grip in his knees that he could fairly make a horse groan, and a horse could pitch a short while until he would have to stop to get his breath. His strength was so great that he could handle the most vicious "bronco" as easily as an ordinary man could a Shetland pony.

Nate Champion (murdered by the cattlemen) was in the employ of the EK outfit, and as Spaugh was not acquainted with the country, Nate was practically in charge of the outfit. When the round-up got as far down Powder river as Davis' ranch, it was joined by Ijams. He stayed with the EK wagon and his stock was gathered and calves branded by Nate Champion.

Ijams had let his cattle to the DV outfit to run that spring, but as the DV only ran a wagon on the Cheyenne river round-up, he had to look after the remnant of his cattle that were on Powder river.

Spaugh and Hesse had several disputes during the general round-up over the tallying. Some of the cattle had been branded very lightly on the shoulder the summer before, and it was very difficult to tell for sure whether an animal that had been branded that way belonged to the trust or the EK outfit. Spaugh was working for the trust, and being an honorable man, wanted to protect his employers. A scratch caused by a hook from the horn of another animal might pass for a dim brand, unless examined closely, so he would require Hesse to rope and throw all suspected animals. This involved a great amount of work, and as Hesse was getting so much the worse of the bargain he got mad and made bluffing talk to Spaugh, but he found his match in every way.

The dishonest work done by Hesse, and the determination of Spaugh to have all the cattle about which there was the least doubt thrown and examined, came near declaring the trade off, but the business was finally settled by the trust buying the cattle on the range. Several head of my cattle were found afterwards with the K tally mark on the shoulder.

When the time came around to begin to hire men in the spring of 1888, Spaugh, who was a stranger, did not know any of the men in the country. One or two of the foremen for other outfits came to him and told him who the black-balled men were, and mentioned several other boys who were not black-balled by the association, but who they had agreed not to employ, and told him that if he wanted to stand in with them (the foremen) he had better not employ these men.

Spaugh did not pay much attention to their talk, but went to Champion, who had been a trusted man in the outfit for a long time and asked him about these men he had been cautioned not to employ. Champion told him who they were, and that they had been accused of branding mavericks, but that he knew of no reason why he should not give them work, as they were the best cow hands in the country and would do good work for him.

So Spaugh, acting on this advice told the foremen who were against these men that he would employ men to suit himself and they could do the same.

These men were George Gordon, George Peterson, Ranger Jones and A. Allison. It was a settled question that I could not work for any outfit, so I went to Spaugh and asked him if he would allow men to go with his wagon and gather my cattle. He told me that I could; that he had been give no instructions in regard to representatives going with him.

So I put my horses in his bunch and my bed in the wagon. When Spaugh started out he had a fine outfit. All of the best men in the country were working for him. It is customary when a general round-up starts in a district, for outfits that belong in other districts to send a man or two to look after what cattle may have strayed off during the winter from their respective districts.

These men came with their string of eight or ten horses and a bed, and they generally are the best men from their outfits and try to throw in with the best outfit in the district they go to.

The boys who came from other districts to the Powder River district, after sizing up the other outfits, concluded to throw in with Spaugh, and as they were supposed, looking out for their outfit's cattle, to make a hand for the outfit they go with, that made Spaugh's outfit pretty strong and independent.

Hesse, with his usual conversation for the interests of the 76 company came out with an outfit composed for the most part of English tenderfeet who had come over to take some lessons in cow-punching and economy under his instructions, with a view to starting in the business for themselves.

A great many young fellows have actually paid such men as Hesse as high as $500 for the privilege of working through the summer, in order to get experience. The balance of Hesse's outfit was made of $30 men, who had probably worked at the business for a year or two.

A fine time they had of it; some of the men hardly knew how to saddle their horses, and as the horses were fat and feeling good from the long lay-over on account of wet weather, they would pitch these tenderfeet off as fast as they could mount, and loose horses with saddles and no riders were running all over the country, keeping those men who could have done any good busy chasing these run-aways.

Some of these could not be caught at all, and now and then a tenderfoot would be minus a saddle, and would have to ride in the mess wagon until he could get another.

I heard some boy call to an Englishman who had been thrown, "Hello, Cully! What did you let him throw you for?" The Englishman replied, "E 'id 'is 'ed h' elevated 'is 'ind parts and I couldn't keep my seat, you know. Blast the bloody brute, h'ill go back to H'england."

Thus it was all through the round-up; the 76 would lose cattle faster than they could gather them. When these "feet" would be sent on herd, they would have to "take a nap you know."

As soon as Hesse saw the men that Spaugh had employed, he began to scheme, not only to have the men fired, but to have Spaugh fired with them. He did not scheme in vain, for just as soon as the round-up was over the general manager of the trust, George W. Baxter, came up and fired the whole outfit, and put John Pierce, one of Hesse's satellites in charge.

That was a splendid change for Hesse, for he could make Pierce handle all of the 76 cattle in the Powder River country and just send a man or two with him, thus saving the expense of a wagon.

Hesse, who had been working for the 76 for quite a while, had improved a large ranch of 640 acres, ditched it, fenced it and built a big house and barn. He also stocked it with machinery, self-binding reaper, mowing machines, gang plows, and in fact latest machinery of all kinds.

Beside this home ranch he had fenced in several thousand acres of land adjoining with a four wire fence, had built miles of expensive irrigating ditches and had four and five men working for him nearly all the time at $40 per month, while he had been getting not more than $2,000 a year as foreman of the 76. He had, beside this, bought quite good a herd of horses and owned a good many cattle.

In 1887 George Harris of Trabing was compelled to sell some of his horses to pay himself out of debt; they were sold at public auction and Hesse bought them. Harris sold 76 head in all. At the time of the sale 70 head were turned over to Hesse, Harris' brand was counter-branded, and Hesse's brand put on them.

An agreement in writing, signed by George Harris and attested to by two parties present, to the effect that Harris would turn over to Hesse the other six head of stock as soon as gathered, as they were running the range. Hesse was perfectly satisfied with the arrangement.

The stock sold by Harris were ordinary range mares and geldings. He had fifteen head of mares which were of a much higher grade, part of them belonging to his children. He was pasturing these 15 head in H. W. Devoe's pasture, drove this stock out and branded four head of them, venting Harris' brand. One of Devoe's men saw Hesse's men driving the stock out of the pasture and went straightaway and told Harris, who saddled his horse as quickly as possible and came up to Hesse's ranch, but he was too late. The mares were already branded and turned out on the range. Harris, was of course, very indignant and was going to have Hesse arrested for stealing his stock, but Hesse begged off and Harris was good natured enough to compromise with him.

That was the clearest case of horse stealing ever known in Johnson county. Harris has since found one or two of his mares that had been vented and Hesse's brand put on the, but the brand had become old and as he had allowed his brand to be vented he could not make a case of it.

The mavericks were sold as usual in 1888 to the highest bidder, but there were not very many of them. The summer of 1888 was a very wet one and grass in consequence was plentiful, hay could be cut in every draw and low place, and even on the hills the grass grew nearly knee deep. The cattle that were shipped in the fall were fat and prices advanced slightly. Stock started into the winter in better shape than they had for years, and there was every reason to think that the loss would be very small.

The country had by this time settled up, until there were a good many families in visiting distance of each other, and the married women, as well as the young girls began to cast about for some way to break the monotony of the long winters and promote social intercourse.

The old-time country dance was the medium through which this could be attained, so about once a week there would be one at some one of the ranches.

There would be no formality connected with them, everybody was expected and everybody generally came. The women brought the eatables, which were always of the best kind, baked meats of all kinds, chickens, cakes, pies, etc. The boys chipped in and paid for music which was always very good, generally comprising three pieces; dancing was always kept up until sun-up and everyone would have a first-class time.

The largest dance given in the winter of 1888-89 was at the now celebrated TA ranch. It was a large roomy house; had just been built, and the floors were smooth and nice to dance on. Charley Ford, who had only been married a short time, acted the genial host to perfection; and it seems strange that three years afterward he should be barricaded in that same ranch house, with 47 other murderers, fighting nine out of every ten men who were there that night.

The winter of 1888-89 was a very mild one, grass was plentiful and cattle generally were fat all the winter, but the spring started in very dry and was backward. The round-up started, as usual at the head of north fork of Powder River the 20th of May.

The 76 company, during the winter, negotiated a sale of their cattle to Weibau of Montana. The conditions of the sale were that they have two years in which to deliver them, 7,000 to be delivered the first year, and 3,000 the second; the price to be $18.50 per head, a cow and a calf going as one head. They had paid from $40 to $60 for their original herd, and in 1883 claimed 80,000 head.

There was one more wagon added to round-up that spring. I had been out to so much trouble gathering my cattle that I determined to start a wagon. I had before this sold to Martin Tisdale, Lou Webb, Thomas Gardner and W. H. Hill each a one-fifth interest in the Hat brand which I owned I had bought the brand from W. E. Hathaway of Powder River in the fall of 1886, it had been on record in Buffalo for two years prior to that time.

We each of us owned a string of horses, and we had a team and wagon, and so, as we only had to hire a cook, we concluded that the cheapest way would be to put a wagon on the round-up.

No rain fell during May and June to speak of and the feed was very poor. The round-up worked south until it met the Platte River round-up. That round-up was in charge of Mike Shaunsey, who was also foreman for the

C Y outfit (J. M. Carey). It seems that Shaunsey had been instructed to blotch all cattle bearing the brand of black-balled men, provided they were not there to prevent it, and to put Carey's brand on them, and also to put M (the association brand) on their neck.

I heard before we met his round-up that he had been doing this, but was told that he had not as yet blotched any of mine. We met his round-up on Salt creek and the two round-ups worked together one day, and then his worked on up and the Powder River round-up worked down Salt creek.

I told him that I had heard about his blotching cattle and asked him if it was true. He told me that he had blotched a few that no owner could be found for. I then told him I did not want him to blotch any of mine, adding tht I would make it warm for him if he did.

He replied, "Oh, no! I will not blotch any of yours, it is a well-known brand an is straight." The next day the round-ups separated and that night a man from Shaunsey's round-up came down to our round-up and told me that he (Shaunsey) had blotched my brand on a yearling and put C Y on it.

The next morning Thos. Gardner and myself went back to the Platte round-up and before I went to Shaunsey I asked several of the boys about the matter, and they all told me that the yearling was perfectly "straight" and was following her cow. I then hunted Shaunsey up and found him at the branding fire and some ten or twelve of his men with him.

I asked him if he had blotched my yearling, and he replied that he had. I said no more but commenced threshing him with my quirt; he attempted to draw his six shooter but dropped it, then he rushed in grappled me, striking me a pretty hard blow on the nose.

I then made an effort to throw him from me when his pants tore loose. That is the sum and substance of my trouble with Shaunsey which the Cheyenne Sun so graphically described. The account given by the Sun was that a crowd of us attacked him, and that he had recovered forty head of stolen Hat cattle for Carey. Afterwards, he did blotch several head more, but gave them up the next spring and vented Carey's brand.

One day about the first of August, 1889, a boy rushed into Casper, Natrona county and said that a man and woman had been hung and that he saw and recognized the parties who hung them. He said the parties who had been hung were James Averill and Ella Watson and the men who hung them were prominent stockmen, their names being Tom Sun, John Durbin, A. L. Rothwell, R. Galbraith and James McLean.

He said that Averill and the woman started from his ranch (Averill's) in a two-horse wagon to go to Casper, that before they got out of the pasture, these men rode up to the wagon, and that from a distance he saw them stop Averill, and then one of them got in the wagon and drove it up into the canyon opening into the Sweetwater canyon.

The boy still followed at a safe distance and saw these men take the man and woman from the wagon, bind the, put ropes about their necks and hang them to a tree. The poor woman was begging and pleading for her life, but in vain. For with a course jest, that deacon in the Methodist church, John Durbin, slapped the bound and helpless woman in the face as he threw the rope over the limb, and thus, with their toes touching the ground they were left to strangle slowly to death, while their inhuman murderers, sat calmly by and gloated over the agony of their victims.

My readers, who have never heard of that circumstance, will very naturally ask: "Is this truth, or is it fiction?" They say, "It can't be true, men who rank high in the social and financial world, could not be guilty of such crimes." But it is true, every word of it, and the adage, "Truth is stranger than fiction," is clearly exemplified in this case.

These men were all arrested and put under bond to appear at the next term of the district court at Rawlins, but before the grand jury convened, this boy, who was the only witness, came up missing, and has never since been seen, or heard of, and the jury returned to bills.

A bleached skeleton was found some time afterwards, and there is every reason to believe it was that of the witness whom these gentlemen (?) murdered, in order that he might not testify against them.

I was in Casper a few days after the arrest of those men, and was told that the people there were terribly excited when the news of the lynching was brought in, and that if some man had taken the lead, the whole town would have followed and killed the last one of the murderers.

The man Averill was a quiet, unobtrusive man and owned no cattle, with the exception of two or three milk cows. He was, at the time of his death, postmaster at Sand creek, and was a surveyor. He had a few years before, while a soldier at Fort McKinney, killed a man in Buffalo, but was honorably acquitted.

The reason for murdering him was the direct result of trouble he had with Bothwell over some fine meadow land that Bothwell was holding illegally.

Averill, being a surveyor, had detected the fraud, and had contested Bothwell's right to the land, and the contest had been decided in his favor only a short while before he was hung.

The woman, it is true, belonged to the demimonde, but she was a woman just the same. She was living with Averill as his wife, and owned about forty head of cattle. After brutally hanging her, they took her cattle, sold them, and kept the proceeds, and this by the representative and reputable men of the country. God help the disreputable ones!

Adding Up the Score

This is the first chapter in the series of atrocities committed by the much-abused cattlemen in Wyoming. We have one man, a woman and a boy murdered, and presuming that every hoof of cattle they owned were stolen, we have 43 head of cattle to balance the lives of three human beings, and one of these a witness only.

The general round-up got through work the last of June in 1889. The summer was hot and dry. Court convened in Buffalo at that time, and the grand jury returned 54 indictments against Al Allison, L. A. Webb, Thomas Gardner, W. S. Hill, William Carroll and myself and the charge was "branding mavericks."

Warrants were placed in the hands of Dick Kennedy, deputy sheriff to serve. Before he got around to serve them some of us came to town.

I heard on my way that Kennedy was looking for me to arrest me, so I came into town and reported to Sheriff Angus. Kennedy, in the meanwhile, went on down to Powder River to arrest Hill, Webb and Gardner. He had been told before leaving town that the case was a desperate one, that the men he was going to arrest would never give up to an officer of the law.

Kennedy was only slightly acquainted with the boys and he thought that what he had been told was true. So he and a deputy left town with six-shooters and Winchesters, and also with many injunctions from their friends to be sure and get the "drop" on the boys or they would surely be killed.

They started from town early in the morning and rode to Terrence Smith's house on north fork of Powder River, where they stayed all night. The boys were at Gardner's ranch, one mile below, on the river. Kennedy was on his horse, and riding toward the rendezvous of the men, who, unless taken by surprise would undoubtedly give him a fight.

The boys had been so accustomed to riding early on the round-up that the habit had become a fixed one, and the smoke curling from the chimney indicated to Kennedy, that, though he was an early bird, he might not have such an easy job catching his worm after all.

But he had started and so must at least make an effort. The boys were all inside of the house cooking breakfast, and they did not see or hear Kennedy as he approached. He got off his horse and stepped to the open door with his gun. Looking up, Webb noticed him.

Boys Are Friendly

"Why, hello Kennedy," he said. "What brings you out this way so early in the morning?"

"I have some warrants for you fellows and came out to arrest you," Kennedy replied.

"Yes," replied Webb; "we heard that there were some warrants issued for us and we were getting an early breakfast, as we were going to town today. Will you have some breakfast with us?"

Kennedy accepted the invitation to breakfast, and they all sat down to the meal. Breakfast over, Webb said:

"I'll just take your horse Dick, and go out and run ours in, they are just over the hill!"

"All right," replied Dick.

So Webb took his horse and in a few minutes came back with the horses. They saddled up and all came into town together. I am pretty sure that Kennedy did not read the warrants to the boys. We tried to have our cases come up for trial at that term of court, but they were put off until the fall term, and we were each put under $1,800 bonds to appear at that court.

The cowmen were satisfied that they had no case against us, and as the penalty for branding a maverick was six months in the county jail and $100 fine, getting the bond as high as they did, they felt sure we would not be able to give it, and would therefore have to stay in jail until the next court, which would be six months away.

We gave the bond though. To make a long story short, when the cases were called at the next term of court, H. S. Elliot, the county attorney, requested Judge Saufley to throw the cases out of court, and the request was granted.

Those, then, are 54 of the many cattle stealing cases that the cattlemen's organs claims that no convictions could be had on in Johnson county.

John Pierce was foreman of the round-up that summer, and was the witness before the grand jury that returned these bills.

I had cattle on the range that I had as clear a title to as a person could possibly have. Yet I was not allowed to buy a maverick that was put up and sold, ostensibly to the highest bidder, nor was I allowed to claim and brand any for myself, even though they might be ranging within a stones throw of my fence.

These dictatorial autocrats, some of them not owning a foot of land could say, "We have defined our boundary lines; every maverick within the limits of those lines is ours; if your animal gets out of your field unbranded, we will neither allow you to take it; nor will we allow you to buy it; when, according to ur law, it is put up for sale. But then I am digressing.

Impartial History

My object is to give a plain, impartial history of the cattle business, without any data or statistics; only such as my memory affords me. I leave the reader to draw his or her deductions.

The 76 had no trouble in finding the required 7,000 head of cattle to be delivered to Weibau, and by the first of July, they were on their way to Montana. I have forgotten to state that this company had, a couple of years previous to this time, driven 10,000 head of cattle into the British territory.

Kansas and Nebraska had been a fine cow country, but civilization kept driving herds farther north until in 1889 northwestern Nebraska was as far south as cattle in any large herds could be found.

The Bay State Cattle Company had thousands of cattle there, but the country was fast filling up with grangers, and as the law there required that stock had to be herded, it was getting too expensive to have cattle there any longer.

A ploughed furrow as a fence, and stock could be held until damages were paid, if it was caught inside of a man's furrow. This company was having considerable trouble on that score, so it determined to move its cattle to Johnson county, and over 20,000 head were driven into the Big Horn basin and Powder river.

Sheep Move In

The sheep industry was beginning to be an important one in this country by this time. The Sweetwater country was filling up with sheep rapidly and the cattlemen there were beginning to move their cattle to Montana. It is a well established fact that cattle won't stay on a range where sheep are ranging unless they are herded.

They leave a scent that cattle do not like, and they will soon leave a water hole that sheep water at constantly; and this fact, coupled with scarcity of feed caused Durbin to drive his cattle from the state.

He had been one of the heaviest losers of any of the cattlemen. He handled Texas cattle very extensively, and the hard winter of '86 and '87 pretty nearly cleaned him out. I remember working on his range in the fall of '85. He had just turned several thousand head of cattle loose. They had been driven from Texas that summer, and were very poor. Yearlings they were, for the most part, little puny things, hardly as large as a native calf six months of age.

They had been on the trail so long and had become so accustomed to traveling that it had become second nature with them, and just as soon as they were turned loose, they scattered all over the country in large bunches. They would not stop long enough to feed, and they would commence to travel, regardless of the direction they went, and in a week after they were turned loose some of them were 75 miles from where they started.

Weather, Not Rustlers

They traveled back and forth, until the storms of winter found them so weak that it was impossible for them to live through it. That is the way Durbin lost his cattle, and not by the depredations of the rustlers.

The Sweetwater country, seven years ago, was considered one of the finest cattle ranges in the west. Today there is not a herd in it of any size. The UT, 71 and other outfits have moved their cattle out, and sheep have taken their places, and they are a source of more benefit to the country than ever the cattle were.

Large corrals have been built at the town of Casper and thousands of sheep are driven there every spring to be sheared, giving employment to a large force of men. Thousands of dollars worth of wool and mutton are shipped every year, and the money, instead of being taken out of the country, as it was by the cattlemen, and spent in riotous living in the east and in foreign countries, is kept in the country.

Cattlemen have always been very aggresive to sheepmen in Wyoming, and have always been loud in their denunciations of them, but just as the lesser force has to give way to the greater, so has the cattle industry had to give way to the greater industry to farming and sheep raising.

Gradually, mile by mile, it has been moved north and west through Kansas and Nebraska until northern Wyoming is its southern limit, and in a few years large herds of cattle in Johnson county will be a thing of the past, and their place will be taken by sheep.

In June, 1889, J. A. Tisdale, who was murdered last November, came to Johnson county. He came with his wife and two little children from Mandan, Dakota, where he had been in the employ of the railroad for some time. His outfit consisted of a wagon and three head of stick. He had two mares that were very fine, weighing about 1,700 pounds each and a saddle horse. Besides this he had $1200 in money, the proceeds from some land that had been sold for him in Texas and money he had saved in Dakota. He moved onto a place on Powder River owned by his brother, and trade his mares for cattle, the mares being valued at $500.

All of the old cattlemen were leaving the country by this time. Peters, Frewen, Plunkett, Roach, Winn and Windsor had all left, and Hesse, foreman of the 76, was handling the cattle owned by these men. They were closing out as fast as they could, and were turning remnants of their herds over to Hesse to dispose of.

The feed was very poor on the range in 1889, and beeves were not fat in the fall. The Hat outfit sold their first beeves that fall, twenty head of long twos, and short threes, and the price received was $18 per head, Speckbasher Bros. of Buffalo being the purchasers.

In the winter of 1889 Capt. Torrey of the M Bar outfit and Spackeman of the open V outfit were both delinquent on taxes to Johnson county, and the county commissioner ordered the treasurer to collect them. Torrey, who claimed that he paid his taxes to Fremont county, was not in the country at the time, being in the East; and as no attention was paid to the treasurer's demand for the taxes, he sent an outfit out to gather sufficient cattle to be sold, to liquidate his indebtedness to the county.

Torrey's cattle ranged on the Big Horn River in the western part of the county. An outfit in charge of Charles Carter was sent over to gather the stock. The cattle were supposed to be sold at public auction in front of the court house at Buffalo.

Several parties who had money intended to be present at the sale, and, if the stock did not sell for too much, buy some of them. The cattle were gathered, the range was culled and only the finest cattle were gathered, principally the fine four and five year old beeves. They were started toward Buffalo, and on the other side of the mountain several of the parties came to the place of sale to buy.

Milo Burke was one of them, and he bought several hundred dollars worth and offered a certified check on the North Platte Bank as payment. Carter, who had charge of the sale, refused to accept the check, saying that he had to have the cash, although Burke assured him that he would have the money for him in 48 hours.

Hesse was the only man from this part of the country who was present, and no one could find out where the cattle were, and he was the only bidder against Burke. It was a pre-concerted plan between Carter and Hesse that the cattle were to be sold to no one except himself, the fact that Carter would not sell them in small numbers to men over there who had cash, substantiating any doubt of the unfairness of the transaction.

The cattle were then moved over the mountain to the NH ranch. A notice of the sale was tacked over the door of the blacksmith shop, and the next day the whole number of cattle, comprising nearly 500 head of fine cows and calves, and beef steers that were worth $49 a head, were knocked off to Hesse for from $5 to $7 a round.

Suit was brought against the county treasurer by Torrey to recover $15,000 damages, and an injunction was put upon the sale of any of the cattle Hesse had bought. The suit is still in litigation.

The legislature convened at Cheyenne on the fourteenth day of January, 1890, and some very peculiar laws were passed. Sec. 1, Chapter 53, of the revised laws passed by the eleventh legislature assembly reads: "The governor of the Territory during the present session of the legislature, and at each session thereafter, shall nominate, and by and with the advise and consent of the legislative council, appoint a board of commissioners, to be known as the board of livestock commissioners of Wyoming."

Sec. 2: "Said board of livestock commissioners shall be composed of five members who shall be the actual owners of livestock, or the owners of stock in any company or corporation having livestock running at large upon the public lands in the territory, and who shall be residents of the territory."

Sec. 3: "Said livestock commissioners shall hold their offices for the term of two years, and until their successors shall be duly appointed and shall have qualified."

Sec. 4: "Said commissioners shall before entering upon their duties, take an oath to uphold the constitution of the United States and the laws of the territory, and to well and truly perform their duties as provided by law, which oaths shall be filed in the office of the secretary of the territory."

Sec. 25: "It shall be the duty of the livestock commissioners, by its secretary or other person selected by it, under its rules, to sell all mavericks in the territory at public auction to the highest responsible bidder offering the highest price per head, at the capitol building of the territory on the first Wednesday after the first Tuesday of each year."

Sec. 35: "The secretary of the commission, shall, within a period of ten days after the receipt by him of the monies paid into his hands on account of the sale of mavericks, transmit the same to the territorial treasurer, who shall give his receipt therefore to the secretary of the commission and deposit the same to the general fund of the territory."

Before the passage of this law mavericks had brought ten dollars per head and the money went into the association fund, and went to defray the running expenses of a club that was run to a grand and sumptuous scale.

The proceeds from the sales over the whole territory amounted to many thousands of dollars. The poor granger, whose calf had probably been stolen by these barons, could look on and ask for enough of the wine--that was flowing like water at their feasts--to wet his lips, but the luxury would be denied him.

Sec. 52: "For the purpose of the livestock commission, as defined and provided for in this act, for the year ending March 31, 1891, the sum of ten thousand dollars is hereby appropriated out of any funds in the territorial treasury not otherwise appropriated."

This, as must be admitted, was certainly a very liberal donation, but, then the state was going to be compensated by the money from the mavericks, at ten dollars per head, but miribilili dictu! when, as provided by the law, the maverick sale came off at Cheyenne, in April, no one of the barons were particular about buying; there were not bidders, and ONE DOLLAR per head was really as much as a maverick was worth; so they knocked down at that amazingly low figure.

The winter of '89 and '90 passed slowly away, and May found the wagons once more on the north fork of Powder preparatory to starting one more general round-up. The 76 had to gather and drive to Montana the balance of the cattle required to fill its contract with Wibau and the Bar C had sold its cattle and was going to drive them north.

The EK was buying Texas steer cattle and bringing them into the Powder River range. After the law which was passed regarding the maverick, causing them to go to the state was passed, the same indifference was shown on the range as was shown in Cheyenne in regard to them.

Hereafter, foreman had been instructed to be sure and get every one of them in on the general round-up, and even after the general, on the summer and fall round-ups, the mavericks were sold for ten dollars.

After the passage of that law very great indifference was shown, they were not so particular as they had been to have them come in for after the general, no more mavericks were sold, they branded them as they came to them and no record was kept for the state.

After Wibau received his number of cattle the remnant of the 76 herd was to be sold to the highest bidder, on the range, Wibau having the option. Wibau concluded to take all that could be gathered over and above his contract number, during the general round-up, at the same figure he took the first, decided that he would try and have the range worked as clean as he could.

Wibau's representative tried hard to have a clean work on the range, but did not succeed very well. After the round-up was through and the cattle all pretty well bunched on the north boundary of the 76 range, preparatory to counting and starting for Montana, someone told Wibau's representative that Hesse's men had driven a bunch of cattle back the day before and had turned them loose about ten miles from where the main bunch was held, so he went back to see about them and found over 400 beeves that had been loose in one bunch.

It transpired soon afterwards that Hesse was negotiating for the remnant.

Arthur Organ asked me if I would be willing to take the remnant of the 76 herd after Wibau had taken his cattle out. I told him I did not think a person would lose anything to take them for 1,500 head, and everyone who had worked on the range for any length concurred with me. Hesse did buy the remnant.

As stated in the last chapter of this review, Hesse bought the remnant of the 76 herd, at least he is supposed to have bought it, as he handled the stick, and was present at the place of sale when it was sold, which was Omaha.

The stock has since been given into the assessor in the names of Windsor and Kemp, but Hesse is known in this country as the owner of the cattle. Hesse's arbitrary and domineering ways were fully demonstrated that summer and the farmers on Crazy Woman and Beaver creek were the sufferers.

By building about two miles of wire fence he completely fenced in some four or five thousand acres of government land. That piece of country the farmers depended upon for a winter range for their small bunches of horses and cattle, as it joined their ranches.

Hesse, after he ran this cross fence, turned the 76, Bar C, Bar X Bar, FU, WP, and all the cattle he was handling into this piece of country, and in a short time he had almost 4,000 head of cattle ranging against the fences, and almost in the doorways of these farmers, and in a short time all of the grass was completely eaten off and the farmers had to let their stock go a long distance from home in order for them to get any feed.

This act of Hesse's was not only unjust, but it was an illegal one, and showed his utter disregard for the interests, as well as for the feelings of the small ranchmen.

The cattle that were put in that enclosure were cattle that did not belong in that neighborhood, their owners had never the least claim on the country as their range. It was done in order to save the expense of a few herders. By the time the grass was eaten off, Hesse was ready to start the cattle north, and the farmers could go and hunt for grass.

In the spring of 1890 the owners of the Hat brand of cattle decided to gather them all and divide them, the agreement being that Allison, Gardner and myself would each take eighty head and Webb and Hill would retain the brand.

We gathered the stock on the general round-up, and right away divided them. Each of us got 35 2-year-old steers, 30 cows, 11 yearlings and four 2-year-old steers. I sold my steers to W. F. Williams, the county treasurer, and 15 head of cows I sold to J. G. Oliver of Buffalo. Allison sold his cows to W. J. Thom, cashier of the First national Bank of Buffalo, and his steers to W. F. Williams.

That left me with fifteen cows and eleven yearlings as my share of the Hat brand, the brand that has been the bane of the cowmen for several years; the brand they claimed had 2,500 head of cattle in it, and they all stolen.

By actual count a few head over 500 head of cattle were rounded up. When the cattle were sold Frank Canton was at the place of sale, where they were branded and turned over, and he claimed that he never saw a straighter bunch of cattle.

There never has been, since the brand had been on the range, a single complaint of any crookedness made against any of the owners. The cases of crookedness on Hesse'a part, that amounted to down-right stealing, are too numerous to mention, but I will cite a few that came under my personal observation, and that will be remembered by many a man still in the country.

A few years ago, I disremember the year, a cow bearing the Bar FS on the right side, and 76 and QT on the left side, was found on the range. The Bar FS was owned on the Belle Fouche by a Mr. Knight. Knight's foreman claimed the cow and took her to his range on the Belle Fouche. Hesse retrieved the cow and brought her back to the 76 ranch, and she was put in the pasture, to await the decision of the court.

In the meantime, Hesse wanted a beef to kill, and as this cow was fat he had her killed, remarking at the time, "I will just settle this case right here." He told Knight's foreman afterwards that the cow got out of the pasture.

Morton Frewen's brother, Dick Frewen, had a band of horses in Johnson county several years ago, he moved them in 1884 lower down Powder River, about to the Montana line. In 1889 one of them, a gray mare, came back to this range, and got into a bunch of Hesse's horses. She had a colt. When the bunch she was in was brought into the ranch at branding time, Hesse put his brand, 28, on the colt, and turned them out together. In 1890 the mare had another colt, and his brand was put on that one also. Frewen's brand was Bar V, and the mare may still be with Hesse's stock.

The first maverick brand started in Johnson county was started in the spring of 1883 by Fred Hesse and C. Ford. It was J-9 brand. Hesse, who was foreman for the 76, expected to be let out that spring, and as mavericks were very plentiful, he and Ford concluded to start a brand. They went out before the general round-up started into the Salt creek and South Fork areas, and they made quite a good branding. They did not lack for good horses to ride, as they had the 76 bunch to pick from.

Their excuse for going out before the general round-up was, that they were looking for horses. When the directors of the 76 outfit met that spring, Moreton Frewen was installed as general manager, and as he thought a great deal of Hesse, he retained him as foreman.

When the round-up caught the yearlings that had been branded J-9, no one claimed them, although Hesse made close inquiries for an owner, and he showed his (?) loyalty to the 76 outfit by putting their brand on them. He knew that he would lose his position if he claimed them himself, because one of the iron clad rules of the cattle barons in those days was, that no man could work for them who owned cattle.

When I bought a few cattle in 1887, Hesse remarked in the presence of County Surveyor Shannon, referring to me, "The son of a b---h, I will have him looking through bars in a year," and although he tried every way in his power to bring about that result, I must chronicle the fact of his being the first to get into that unenviable position, and I hope that if I ever do "look through bars," it will not be for committing as cold-blooded and cowardly a murder as he committed.

Although somewhere in the neighborhood of 3,000 head of 76 cattle were gathered in the spring of '83 for Wibau and the number left on the range was supposed to have been about 1,500, only 2,200 head were given in to the assessor for taxation. Hesse had bought the fall before this, between four and five hundred head of cattle sold for delinquent taxes, and had besides these a good many others, still the number of head given in by him for taxation in 1890 was 300.

There was a two-fold object in putting in the 76 cattle at such a few head, and the main one was to hoodwink the owners and give them to believe that the remnant was very small, and certainly no one could have any object in representing the remnant to be very small, only one contemplating buying it.

In the fall of 1890 the first state officers of the new state were elected. Frances E. Warren was elected governor and Amos W. Barber, a one-horse doctor, was elected secretary of state. A very short time after his election to the highest office within the gift of the people in a state, Governor Warren resigned to accept the U.S. senatorship and Barber became acting governor. In Johnson county, although strongly opposed by the cattlemen, W. G. Angus was elected sheriff. John N. Tisdale, one of the murderers now confined in Fort Russell was elected state senator. He was present at the first session of the state legislature in Cheyenne.

A short time afterwards he sold out his interest in Johnson county and went to Salt Lake City, where he engaged in the real estate business, never having resigned his position as senator. The next time he was seen in Johnson county was when he surrendered with 47 other murderers at the famous TA ranch. H. W. Davis was elected to the legislature and claims the honor of being the framer of the bill that repealed the maverick law, thereby making mavericks public property.

He went to Cheyenne a short while before the invasion of the county by the cattlemen. When the invaders left Cheyenne he was with them, and came with them to the ranch of Robert Tisdale, the place where they recruited their energies wasted by the long ride from the railroad preparatory to making the attack on the ranch where they knew two unsuspecting men were sleeping.

There, our county's representative in the legislature lost his courage, and with Ed Towse, the Cheyenne Sun reporter, and Dr. Penrose of Philadelphia, the surgeon of the expedition, he slipped off and was probably not missed by the leaders, who, from all account, filled themselves with whiskey before starting on their mission of death. He made his way from there to his ranch and since then has never been heard of. It is claimed that he made his way out of the country dressed in woman's clothes.

These men are still holding their offices and unless Tisdale resigns and allows the voters to elect a man to fill his place there will be a vacancy in the upper house and the next legislature will have to throw him out.

Anyone who was in Johnson county as early as '82 or '83 and then left, coming back now, would not recognize the country. The whole country is completely metamorphised; where formerly the traveler could ride in any direction for days almost, without seeing a fence or a farm, he now finds them every few miles.

Fine hay meadows and fields of waving grain have taken the place of sage brush flats and barren hillsides. The mournful howl of the coyote and wolf have been succeeded by the far sweeter sounds of the ranchman's song and the prattle of children. Small herds of horses, cattle and sheep have taken the place of the large herds of the barons that have been forced to leave the county on account of the curtailing of the ranges by the fences and farms of the farmers.

Many and loud have been the mutterings and threats made by the cattlemen as they saw the rich grazing lands of the government slipping acre by acre from their grasp although they had resorted to various unlawful ways to hold it.

The season of 1890 saw a great many cattle removed from the state; nothing of any note transpired. The winter was a mild one and the loss on stock was very small.

The season of 1891 was approaching; the season of bloody murders committed by the stockmen and their hired assassins. The grand document of the bloody plots of the cowmen was to soon be enacted and the world was soon to be staggered by accounts of their foolhardy fiendishness, and the virgin state of Wyoming was soon to experience the throes of warfare, and prove the loyalty and love of her citizens for right and justice.

The storm that had been gathering for years was soon to break, and out of its dark bosom a band of treacherous murders was to descend upon a peaceable community and the bosom of mother earth to be stained with the blood of their victims.

May, 1891, once more came around. May, that most pleasant of all the months in Wyoming, with sunshines and invigorating breezes, laden with the perfume of flowers that everywhere are just beginning to raise their timid heads as though inviting the bee to come and sip the honey from their lips.

The trees, putting forth their summer coat of verdure, are swept gently by the wind, and their leaf-clad boughs offer rest and shade to joyful birds, pouring forth the welcome to spring in volumes of sweet song.

The feeling is contagious, it is caught up by all life, animate and inanimate. Horses neigh, cattle low, and the young calves are seen playing around their more sedate mothers and wondering why they do not show their joy and appreciation of the glorious spring in the same frolicsome way that they do. The mothers are enjoying the sweet, fresh grass, which they have so long been deprived of, and that tastes so good to them after brousing on the dry tasteless feed of the winter.

The boys have had enough of winter, they are tired of dancing and frolicking, and are glad the time has come for them once more to roll up their beds, saddle their fat horses and resume round-up work.

The legislature convened at Cheyenne the winter before, and the old maverick law was repealed and mavericks were made public property, as ought to have been the rule always. They belonged to the man now catching them.

There were very few of them in the country, though, as the EK outfit was the only one having many cattle. Most of the large outfits had begun by this time to spay their calves as the best way to close out their herds, which were no longer so profitable, and the EK spayed a great many.

The roundup started as usual on the north fork of Powder river, with two wagons present, the EK and 76, Mike Shaunsey was foreman of the former and John Pierce was foreman of the latter. A new black-ball list had been made out by the Northern Wyoming Protective Association that spring at its meeting, and it included nearly every man in the country who owned a hoof of stock, and the foremen had strict oreders not to allow any of them to eat a meal at their wagons, or to turn one of their cattle, or to allow a man in their employ to assist them in any way in handling their stock.

My name had been on the black-ball list for several years, but for some unaccountable reason it was taken off that spring, and Shaunsey offered to let me go with his wagon and gather my cattle. I had only a few cattle out of my pasture and told Shaunsey that I did not intend to be on the roundup at all, but their the other boys were going to look after and bring in my cattle.

Two or three wrangles came up during this roundup over unfair treatment of the black-balled boys by Pierce and Shaunsey. On one occasion, Nate Champion had four or five head of cattle in Shaunsey's herd that had gotten in accidentally. He went to Shaunsey and told him they were in there and he would like to get them out, as he supposed that he (Shaunsey) did not want them in his herd.

Shaunsey told him that it did not make any difference that he could leave them in and he would hold them for him, that he would work the bunch in a day or so and then he could get them out. As soon as Nate was gone he had the bunch rounded up and cut Nate's out and ran them off.

That, of course, vexed Nate and he had some words with Shaunsey over the matter. Shaunsey never forgave him, though apparently afterwards he was very friendly. He was only nursing his anger and hate which he was too cowardly to show openly, and the night of October 31, 1891, he and five or six other assassins crawled to Champion's door and tried to murder him, but owing to his bravery and presence of mind they were foiled in the attempt. Robert Tisdale, one of the murderers at Russell, also found cause that summer, as he thought to join a conspiracy later on to murder Champion.

The Bar C outfit had for the last ten years claimed as their range a strip of country about thirty miles in length bounded on the west by the Big Horn Mountains, and on the east by a natural rock wall, that for the whole distance of 30 miles only had four openings of which stock could go through, and as none of the openings were over a quarter of a mile wide it was a very small matter to keep them fenced.

The country was open on the south. There was plenty of water in their large, natural government pasture, which contained something like 75,000 to 100,000 acres, and the Bar C had very little trouble handling their cattle which were kept there. As that outfit had taken their cattle from the country, there were not cattle in this pasture, so Champion, having about 200 head of cattle, concluded to throw them in there.

Tisdale had about 2,000 head of cattle and he also had about 50,000 acres of government land that was fenced in. He figured that by putting his cattle in this pasture vacated by the Bar C, that he would not have to turn any of his stock on the range and could keep his pasture at home for winter use. He put his cattle in their large pasture of 100,000 acres, and a short time afterwards, Champion turned his 200 head in the same pasture.

Just as soon as Tisdale knew of Champion having put his cattle in, he began to raise the devil and said that he did not see what right Champion had to put his cattle in where he had his. He blustered around a while and finally rounded his cattle up and drove them out and turned them loose, taking a good many of Champion's with him.

Just for that, and nothing else, he determined that Champion should die, and at once began to take steps to bring about that end.

The EK otufit drove in several thousand cattle during the summer and turned them loose on the north fork. There are several small farmers on that river, and they were not able to fence their farms with the very best fence. Those Texas cattle were a great nuisance to them, they would crowd through the wire fences and destroy their crops in spite of all they could do. On one occasion the 71 outfit was camped on the river close to the home of Mr. A. A. Frame, who was not at home. Frame had a patch of ground of a few acres fenced in for garden, oats, etc.

The grass was pretty well eaten out and it was hard to keep a bunch of horses from running off during the night so the outfit drove their bunch of 50 or 60 horses into Frame's garden patch and left them all night, and the next morning everything was completely eaten and trampled out.

The latter part of June 1891, the report came to Buffalo that Thomas Waggoner had been hung. Waggoner lived in Weston county. He was a horse grower. He had several hundred head of horses and was reported worth $50,000. He was a quiet, unobtrusive man and was well thought of by nearly everyone in the county except the cowmen. He had a wife and two children.

One day, according to his wife's statement, in the latter part of June, three men who were strangers to her, came to the house and arrested Waggoner on a warrant they had.

Waggoner offered no resistance but was perfectly willing to go with them, but seemed surprised at being arrested as he could think of no reason why he should be. He started from home with the men and his wife came running out where they were a few yards away with his pocketbook and told him that he had forgotten it and that he had better take it along, as he might need some money when he got to town.

Little did the poor woman know what little need he had for money or that she was destined never to see him alive again. He was in the hands of demons blacker than any in hell, who would show him no mercy. His appeal to be allowed to see his wife and babies before being murdered was met with scoffs and jeers, and three miles from their presence a rope was put about his neck with the other end thrown over a limb, his horse was driven from under him and he was left to slowly strangle to death while his tormentors stood around and gloated over their devilish work.

Can anything more horrible be conceived of? Could any devil in hell perpetrate a more heartless and diabolical piece of cruelty? To just think of it! These men cooly, calculatingly and for a few dollars paid by the cowmen, take a man who has never done them any harm in the world, away from his wife and little children and strangle him to death.

The cowmen undoubtedly had their work done for why should the men charged with doing the work have done it? It was not done from any personal motive or revenge or hate on the part of the men doing it but purely for money;

money offered by the cattlemen for having that kind of work done. And those are the men confined at Fort Russell, who the Sun and Tribune are holding up to the world as "abused gentlemen."

The wife of Thomas Waggoner anxiously awaited the return of her husband after leaving with the three men. The hours grew into days, and days into week, and still he came not. The poor woman was frantic. The country around was very thinly settled and she could hear nothing of her husband. Inquiry established the fact that he had never appeared in Newcastle, the county seat of Weston county, and the people became alarmed as they began to fear that he had met with foul play. The twelfth day after he left home his body was found hanging to the limb of a tree in an out-of-the-way gully. It presented a horrible appearance; the face was black and swollen beyond all recognition and the rope had cut deep into the mortified flesh of the neck.

H. B. Ijams was up in this country a short time after Waggoner's death, and at Sage creek station on his return to Cheyenne, he was heard to say, speaking of Waggoner:

"We have hung one of the son's of b---s and we will get some more of them, and their families won't save them."

Last winter this same man, Ijams, was in Idaho hiring men to come on this last raid to Johnson county to murder settlers. The Waggoner death ends the second chapter in the series of murders done by the cattlemen and their hired assassins.

In the last chapter of this review I told of the hanging of Tom Waggoner by the cowmen. In spite of the fact that circumstantial evidence pointed pretty plainly to more than one man who had a hand in the crime, nothing was ever done about it.

There was no positive evidence upon which to arrest anyone, but people did not hesitate to say who they thought were the guilty parties. The murder was planned and executed in a way that left no trail, and in a short time had even ceased to be talked of and was charged to the cattlemen.

The grass crop of 1891 was very good but cattle did not get fat. The reason was on account of the great number of Texas cattle and so few native cattle being on the range. Texas cattle were very wild and were continually on the run. Whenever they would see a man on horseback they would start on a run and it required a good horse to round a bunch of them up, and if not rounded up they would go ten or twelve miles before stopping.

The consequences was that when shipping time came they, and the native cattle, too, were very poor. The EK shipped a great many of those poor beeves and they brought a very low figure.

A few cattle were shipped by the black-balled boys in the fall of 1891, and the money was all held by the stock commission. Ijams, the secretary of the commission, was in Omaha and whenever a bunch of black-balled cattle were loaded at any of the shipping points, he was immediately notified by telegram by one of his secret agents. As soon as the cattle were unloaded and put into the feeding pens at Omaha, a complaint was made that they were stolen cattle, and the sheriff took charge of them. They were then sold and the money turned over to the stock commission.

Parties shipping the cattle were told that when they furnished the proof that the cattle belonged to them the money would be paid over. Proof was furnished in the shape of bills of sale, and affidavits attested by good responsible parties, but no money was forthcoming. The commission stated that it still needed more proof of ownership. One of the brands of cattle held by the commission was the Hat.

As stated before, W. F. Williams, the treasurer of Johnson county, had, two years before, bought a lot of these same Hat cattle, and at the time they were sold Fred Hesse also tried to buy them, but could not. Mr. Williams shipped the Hat steers that he had bought and they were not stopped by the commission. When Lou Webb and William Hill, who owned the brand, shipped theirs, they were stopped and their money held.

The brand is one of the oldest in the state, and has been on record in the county clerk's office for eight or nine years. All this proof together with the bill of sale, was sent to the secretary of the commission, and they still held the money. Several thousand dollars in all is thus withheld from Wyoming men who shipped cattle to Omaha.

The scheme was so secretly worked by the thieving commission that no one had an opportunity to take any counter action, and as the shippers were all poor men they were not able to take any legal steps right away.

The cases have now been put in the hands of a competent lawyer and there is not the least doubt of the cases being won by the shippers, together with the damages.

Right away after taking this money from the boys in this county, the cowmen began to form their plans to murder some of them, as then they could hold the money and there would been no one left to prosecute the cases against them.

It seems to be pretty well substantiated that a paper was taken around to the cowmen for them to sign, each signer putting so much money against his name, the same to be 'blood money' to be paid the man or men who would murder a black-balled man. I have been told that the paper was brought to J. E. Shannon, the county surveyor of Johnson county, for him to sign and he refused to sign it.

A man in Gillette says he will swear that Ijams offered him $5,000 to kill men, and that he told Ijams to put up the cash, and he would do the work for him. He says that Ijams refused to put up the cash but told him he would have no trouble getting the money after the work was done. But the offer was declined. Men were then found, though, who did accept the offer and immediately set about earning their money.

The small stockowner then determined for their mutual benefit to organize and form for their protection, an association. A great many of them claimed that the large owners had been driving out of the country and shipping their stock from time to time.

There is a law on the statutes that makes it a fineable offense for an outfit when moving cattle, to drive off of its range an animal belonging to another party. The big outfits had never respected the law, and had time and again driven cattle off in their herds that they would be moving thru the country, belonging to farmers, and turned them loose many miles from their owner's range.

In the majority of cases these cattle would never be recovered and on the range where they were turned loose, no owner could be found for them when they would be rounded up the next year, as the farmers owning them would not be able to have a representative on the different round ups looking out for them, and they would be called strays and would be shipped and the money turned into the association.

The object of the farmers and small stock growers in forming an association was mainly to guard against that way of losing their stock. The night of Oct. 30 was set as the time for holding the meeting in Buffalo to organize.

About all the stock owners were present, and the by-laws having been read nearly everyone present joined. John R. Smith was elected president and Dr. J. C. Watkins, secretary and treasurer. The by-laws required every member to report any crookedness seen on the range to the association, and any one of the big outfits found driving stock off the range was to be prosecuted. Nearly every man in the Powder river country was present at the meeting except Nate Champion and Ross Gilbertson.

A few days before this meeting, Joe Elliot, who is one of the men suspected of helping to hang Tom Waggoner, was in Buffalo. He claimed he was a deputy sheriff and was after some horses that were supposed to be north, that the Waggoner estate held a mortgage on. He told Deputy Sheriff Roles that he was going north. Roles did not see him anymore, but that day Sheriff Angus met him going south, leading a horse, packed with bedding, etc.

Champion and Gilbertson lived in a small log house of one room, on the head of Powder River. The house belonged to W. H. Hall, and they had rented it from him.

In the afternoon of Oct. 31, Nick Ray was riding up Beaver creek on his way to the Riverside postoffice when he noticed two men camped in the bend of the creek. Their horses were grazing around, and Ray recognized one of the horses as belonging to Joe Elliot. It was about three miles from where Ray saw these men camped, to the house of Nate Champion.

The next morning about daylight, Champion who was still in bed, was awakened by having his door suddenly shoved open. Immediately three men sprang into the room and to the foot of his bed.

Champion asked them who they were and what they wanted. One of them replied, "tramps!, and added, "we have got you. you might as well give up."

Champion made no reply, but he reached for his six-shooter, which was hanging in the scabbard on the bed post. Just them one of the men fired, and the pistol was so close to Champion's head that his face was powder burned.

The slight turn of his head in reaching for his pistol was all that saved Champion's life. He got his pistol so quickly and fired, that the two shots were almost simultaneous. Another one of the party then fired, and the bullet went into the bed clothing near the center of the bed, and then the attacking party turned to run out of the room, and two more shots were sent after them.

When they were out of the room, Champion jumped out of bed and ran to the door. As he looked out he saw three or four men running off through the bushes that surrounded the house. He stepped out to get them, and as he did so, a man jumped out from around the corner of the house, and leveled a six-shooter held in both hands, at him.

Champion jumped back inside the door and shot at the fellow who ran around the house and disappeared in the brush.

Champion and Gilbertson then came out of the house and got the guns, and started to go to the Bar C ranch, about one-half mile away. A short distance from the house they found four overcoats that had been left by the would-be murderers.

They followed up the fleeing cut-throats and found their camp within a quarter of a mile of the NH ranch, which proved beyond a doubt that Shaunsey, the EK foreman, was at least cognizant of the purpose of the party if he was not a member of it.

When the camp was found, the party had gone but appearances showed that they left in a great hurry. A considerable portion of their bedding was left behind, together with their cooking outfit. A tarpaulin that was left had considerable blood on it, which was afterwards analyzed and found to be human blood, showing that one of Champion's shots had hit its mark. Near the camp some horses were found and among the number was the black horse that Elliot had packed when Sheriff Angus met him.

Everything pointed so plainly to Elliot's guilt that a warrant was sworn out for his arrest, and he was brought to Buffalo. At his preliminary examination his guilt was proven beyond a doubt. Champion had never seen Elliot to know him before this and he recognized him at once as the man who came around the corner of the house with the pistol leveled at him.

Elliot protested his innocence, but bail was fixed at $5,000 for his appearance at the next term of court. He was only in jail about two weeks until bail was furnished by the stockmen.

It has since been learned that six men were present when the attack was made, and that Mr. Shaunsey was one of them; that he acted as guide for the party, as the location was an out-of-the-way one, and none of the others knew the place well enough to go to it in the night.

The next day after the attack, Shaunsey sent word down to Champion that if he was afraid to stay at his house to come up to the EK ranch and stay, but the invitation was declined.

Champion suspected Shaunsey at once, as he had been there the day before on a pretense of trading horses in order to find out where the band was located, etc. He was foiled that time, but his next attempt cost poor Nate his life.

After the attempt to take the lives of Champion and Gilbertson last fall, all the boys living on Powder river, very naturally, alive to the fact that although foiled in their last attempt to do murder, the cattlemen did not stop, but would resort to some other means to accomplish their aim, which was to murder some of the black-balled men, and therefore intimidate a lot more who they thought would then leave the country.

They would then have all the range to themselves. After the cowardly attempt, everybody went armed, but all the arms a man can carry will avail him nothing, when a coward will be in a gulch and shoot one in the back.

Extra precautions were, nevertheless, taken, and doors were securely fastened at night. But that, too, was a useless precaution, for the murderers profiting by their experience gained in their first attempt, had determined to try a safer plan and not expose themselves to any danger.

They had had enough of breaking in doors and running in on occupants of houses. They had found out that there were brave men in the country, who would not give up to them and be hung like dogs, although having great odds against them.

The plan they determined upon was to wait until men would come into town from their ranches, and they would lie in wait and shoot them from hiding places, as they went home. District court convened the latter part of November and brought a good many people to town. All of the cattlemen were in and then the plot was laid and the plan of operations decided upon.

About the 20th day of November, O. E. Jones, known by the familiar name of Ranger Jones, started to Buffalo. He was building a house for himself on a piece of land he had filed on. He expected to get married in a short time, and was anxious to get his house finished.

His object in going to Buffalo was to see about getting some lumber needed for flooring. He told his brother, whom he left at home, that he would be back in four or five days. Ranger was a young fellow, 23 years of age. He was a jolly, good-natured boy whom everybody liked. He and his brother came to Johnson county in]887, and worked for the cow outfits in the country. They were both very saving and never spent any money foolishly.

Ranger was never known to take a drink of whiskey. The two brothers brought a buggy and a span of horses up from Nebraska with them, and traded them off for some Indian mares, and they afterwards bought a few head of cattle.

To return to the story. When the time for Ranger's return from town arrived and he did not come, his brother began to get uneasy, but still expected him. He waited a day or two longer and then he started out to look for him.

A day or two after Ranger left his home, J. A. Tisdale also started in his wagon to go to Buffalo to get his winter supplies. He also expected to be gone about five days, as he lived sixty miles from town. Tisdale had been in the country several years and had never been known to drink or gamble, or in any way spend money foolishly.

He had a wife and three children, the youngest one not two years old. This time in town he seemed to be worried about something, and did drink a little. He told a friend he had overheard talk that led him to think the cowmen were plotting to kill him. The remark he overheard was made by Frank Canton in a conversation with Hesse, and was to the effect that he (Canton) would tend to him (Tisdale). That remark preyed on his mind and caused him to go to drinking and delayed his departure for home.

Ranger was in town at the same time and started home the afternoon of the 28th day of November. He was in a buckboard and was driving two horses. About fifteen miles from Buffalo, D. A. Kingsbury met him. About one-half a mile before meeting him, Mr. Kingsbury crossed the bridge over a small creek called Muddy, and saw a short distance up the creek, a man with a rifle in his hands, but paid no particular attention to him, thinking he was a freighter looking for his stock.

This was at sundown. A few minutes later he passed Ranger, and was greeted pleasantly by him. The man seen near the bridge evidently had secreted himself under the bridge and waited for Ranger to drive across and then shot him. He was shot three times.

The murderer was not more than six feet away when he fired. The first shot struck a large cartridge belt worn by Ranger, and did no harm. The other two shots were both mortal ones; one in the side and the other in the chest.

There must have been two men present when the shooting was done. The road, twenty feet after leaving the bridge, goes through a short cut between two banks, and in there a man must have stood to stop the team, for one of the horses was a wild one and would have run when the shot was fired, and the man under the bridge could not have caught them. They had been stopped at once, for there were no mark of the buggy or team outside of the road, before entering the cut. After the team was stopped, it was then driven out of the road and there stopped under a bank, and out of sight of the road. The team was unhitched and unharnessed. The horses were taken away and poor Ranger was left there in his buggy, dead. His murderer was gone, leaving no evidence of his crime.

Two days after Ranger left town, John Tisdale prepared to leave. He was still uneasy and suspicious of some impending danger and frequently spoke of it. He had a six-shooter, but before leaving town he bought a double-barreled shotgun and loaded it with buckshot.

He did not get started from town until late in the afternoon, and stopped that night four miles out, at the Cross H ranch.

His murderer started out of town a short distance ahead of him and was met by H. W. Devoe. The weather was very cold and he had a handkerchief tied over his face and Mr. Devoe could not recognize him. It was expected that Tisdale would stop at the Cross H, and the man expected to kill him beyond there, on an unfrequented part of the road, late in the evening.

It was so ordained, though, that there was to be a witness to the murder. Tisdale still showed his uneasiness at the Cross H ranch and that night had the window blinds all closed and told one of the boys there that he thought the cowmen were going to kill him.

He started the next morning on his journey home. When about two miles from his starting place he met the mail carrier coming to Buffalo and stopped and had a short talk with him. One mile further on his murderer was lying in a gulch within twenty feet of the road, waiting for his victim to approach.

Slowly, but surely, Tisdale, with his heavy load was going to meet his death at the hands of the cowardly fiend. He approached, passed, and when twenty-five feet by, the murderer's rifle belched forth its deadly contents. The first shot, from appearances, as in Ranger Jones' case, struck the handle of his coat on the left side, and glanced off. He evidently tried to cock and shoot his gun them, for one of the cartridges was indented slightly, as though he had drawn the hammer back part way, and it had then slipped from his thumb, he having received a death shot in the side, before he had time to fully cock it, and the poor fellow fell back on his load shot to death.

The murderer then took the team and drove it about half a mile below in the gulch and shot both the horses dead.

Providence had so ordained that there should be a witness to this foul deed. Charles Basch, who was coming in to Buffalo at an early hour, rode on to the murderer and was close enough to recognize man and horse.

The man he said he thought was Frank Canton, and the horse was a noted sorrel that he (Basch) knew well, having known the whole time since Canton owned him, and having ridden him. Basch came to town and was overtaken on the road by a man from the Cross H ranch who asked him if he had met Tisdale, and told of what he had seen, and told him that the man who did the deed was riding Canton's horse.

Court was in session and Sheriff Angus sent Deputy Roles and three or four men to bring in the body. One of the party, Thomas Gardner, went to Powder River to take the sad news to the murdered man's family.

He got to my house at 12 o'clock in the night and told of the occurence, rested a few minutes, and then went on to tell the waiting wife of her husband's death.

It was a sad mission to perform. Word was sent from my house to all the families in the neighborhood, and by sunrise all of the boys in the country were at my place, and in the evening everybody had started for Buffalo, arriving there at 12 o'clock in the night.

In the meantime, Ranger Jones' brother had gotten to town and reported his brother's absence, and a crowd started out to search for him and he was found as described.

The crowd that came to town was very orderly and quiet and gave the marshal no trouble. The men were all anxious to have the murderer brought to justice.

Frank Canton and Hesse did not show themselves on the street but remained concealed. Finally word was sent to Canton that the boys wanted to see him and have him explain about his horse having been ridden by the murderer.

Canton sent word down that he would not come; but that if I would come to where he was he would talk to me and explain. I went to see him and he told me that he had not been out of town and neither had his horse, and asked me if his life would be safe in case he went out and saw the boys.

I told him I could not answer for the whole crowd but that I would bring five or six of them up to see him and could answer for them that he would not be hurt.

The boys came up to see him and had a talk, but Canton could not satisfy them as to his innocence.

Canton was given a preliminary hearing before Justice of the Peace

Parmalee, and great many witnesses who were called for the defense swore to the fact that Canton had been in town all the morning from 6 o'clock until noon, and Canton swore that his horse had been in his stable all the morning under lock and key, and had not been out only when he took him to water.

Witnesses for the state swore differently. Basch swore that his horse was at the gulch where Tisdale was murdered. T. B. Hutton, who has since died, swore that he saw Canton come in on his horse, that he spoke to him; that the horse was covered with sweat and foam. Mrs. Conrad swore that she saw a man riding a sorrel horse at tremendous speed coming from the direction of the gulch. In spite of all this evidence Canton was discharged, and in a few days he and Hesse left the country.

Additional evidence was brought up against Canton after he left and another warrant was sworn out for him, but Barber would not make a requisition on the governor of Illinois for him, where he then was. Canton came back to Cheyenne and was there admitted to bail in the sum of $30,000. The next seen of him was when he was arrested at the TA ranch.

Two more men had been killed by the cattlemen and their hired thugs, and still they went free to plan more murders, and on a more wholesale plan.

Shortly after Canton and Hesse left Buffalo, Charley Ford and H. W. Davis left to join the conspirators in their plans for murder. As Frank Canton and Parker were sent to Texas to hire all of the bad characters, who, for five dollars a day, would be willing to join a raid to kill settlers in Johnson county.

H. B. Ijams was sent west to work Idaho and Oregon and gather up all of the same class who could be found in these states willing to kill for money.

Missouri and Arkansas contributed to the gang. The Texas agents were successful in getting some 25 men.

Ijams was not so lucky and did not find many men who were willing to join his nefarious raid. Suffice it to say, though, that a gang of 50 were gotten together, and preparations were begun for the invasion.

Horses, saddles, and the latest improved Winchester rifles were furnished every one, basides a .45 calibre six-shooter, and some had two six shooters. Three wagons were bought, with four horses for each, and they were loaded with bedding, grub, oats, etc.

This outfit was loaded onto cars at Cheyenne and run up to within two miles of Casper. It purported to be a surveying outfit, and as it made the run in the night, did not attract much attention, although some people became suspicious of its real motive and warnings were sent north, but did not arrive, as the telegraph wires were cut.

The outfit unloaded from the cars before daylight, and by sunup was well on its way to Powder river. Their first stopping place of any duration was at the ranch of Robt. Tisdale's where they stayed a day and night and rested up.

The night of April 8th, they all started late at night for the KC ranch where they knew two men, Champion and Ray, were stopping. They got to the KC ranch before daylight, and silently rationed themselves around the ranch in the stable, gulches, etc. and quietly waited for the men in the house to come out.

The first man to come out was an old hunter and trapper, who happened to be stopping at the ranch that night; he and his partner, a young fellow. The

The old man came down to the river out of the sight of the house for water, and was compelled, at the muzzle of a gun, to submit and keep quiet.

His partner waited a while for him to come back, and then started for the river to see what had become of him. He, too, was held up and forced to keep quiet.

The next man to appear was Nick Ray. He came out a few steps from the door, looked around, and then started to walk back into the house. Before he got to the door, two shots rang out and he fell, and then started to crawl into the house, and several more shots were fired at him.

Champion sprang to the door and pulled him inside and shut the door, and for ten hours he held 50 murderers who were clamoring for his life, at bay.

The morning of the 9th, I had started from my ranch, eighteen miles above the river, to go to Douglas. I was on horseback, and my step-son, a boy of 17 years of age, started with me to go to the Powder river crossing.

He was driving two horses and had only the running gear of a small wagon. We got to the CK ranch about 2:30 p.m. I was riding about fifty yards behind the wagon. We could not see the stable behind which the murderers were concealed, until we were within 75 yards of it. When the wagon drove into sight the murderers jumped up and commanded the boy to halt, but he urged up his horses and drove for the bridge. When they saw he would not stop, one of them took aim on the corner of the fence and fired at him. The shot missed him and scared his team, which stampeded across the bridge and on up the road.

There were 20 men behind the stable, and seven came up on horseback, three from one side of the road and four from the other, and closed in around me. When the men behind the stable saw me, they began to jump for their guns, which were leaning against the fence, and called on me to stop and throw up my hands.

I did not comply with their order but kept on straight for the bridge. When I got to the nearest point to them, 47 steps, a man whom I recognized as Ford, stepped from the crowd, and, taking deliberate aim at me with his Winchester, fired.

I threw myself on the side of my horse and made a run for it. The seven horsemen followed me. When I overtook my wagon, which had my rifle on it, I told the boy to hand it to me, which he did. I then told him to stop and cut one of the horses loose and mount him.

The seven horsemen were following me, and when I stopped, were 350 yards behind, but as soon as they saw I had a rifle, they stopped. I only had three cartridges for my rifle, and did not want to fire a one of them, unless they came closer, which they did not seem inclined to do .

The murderers then took the wagon we had left, pulled it back to the KC ranch, loaded it with pitch pine posts, shoved it against the house and set them afire, and the house was soon in flames.

After leaving the KC, we made our way to Trabing, 30 miles away, getting there at 9 o'clock at night. We were recruited with three more men, and started back to the assistance of the men who we thought were still imprisoned at the KC ranch.

We got to Carr's ranch, 17 miles from the KC and there we found 12 more men who had heard the news, it having been conveyed by Terrance Smith, who had heard the firing in the morning and hastened for Buffalo, scattering the news as he went.

Just as we rode up to Carr's ranch, some one exclaimed: "There they are on the flat, 100 strong." This was 12 o'clock at night. Just before we arrived at Carr's ranch the 12 men there had started to go to the KC and had seen the murderers coming and were preparing to ambush them, when one of the boys let his gun go off accidentally, and the murderers swung off to the left and went through Carr's field.

We laid at the ranch till daylight and then followed them up, passing them at the T.A. ranch, and going on to Buffalo. W. G. Angus had, in the meantime, started from Buffalo with a small squad of men for the KC, but we missed him on the way. We were reinforced in Buffalo and started back to the T.A. ranch with 48 men.

We surrounded the ranch at daylight, and a short while afterwards the invaders opened the fight by firing a shot at one of the squads of men about 400 yards off. That was a signal for hostilities to commence, which they did in earnest!

About nine o'clock, three wagons were described coming over the hill two miles away, and some of the boys started back and found them to be the invaders. They were taken possession of and pulled into camp and unloaded. Fuse, giant powder and poison were among the articles found in them. This was on Monday, April 11.

All day Monday recruits kept joining the beseigers, but the beseiged were strongly fortified and it was impossible to rout them. The house was built of sawed logs 10 x 12 laid one upon the other. There were four rooms in the house. The windows were logged up and port-holes cut.

One hundred yards from the house was a log stable, and a short distance from the stable was a log fort, built on a hill that commanded a sweep of 600 yards in every direction. An ice house also made a good fort; all of these places were full of men with the finest kind of repeating rifles, that would carry up for a thousand yards.

Monday night was employed by the besiegers in digging rifle pits, and Tuesday morning they had approached considerably nearer the house.

Tuesday a large force of men joined the besiegers from both the Johnson and Sheridan counties. The construction of a movable fort was begun Tuesday and was ready to be moved up to the breastworks early Wednesday morning. Tuesday night the men worked like beavers. The invaders attempted to make a break for liberty Tuesday night and some of the horses were led out of the stable, but bullets were poured into them so fast and thick that they were glad to get back under cover.

Wednesday morning the situation was anything but pleasant for the invaders. The pits had been dug to within 300 yards of the house and the movable breastworks was ready to be moved forward; in fact it had been manned and was moving, when the bugles were heard and the soldiers came into sight, and in a few minutes the invaders had surrendered.

They were taken away from the sheriff, marched to Fort McKinney where they were confined for a few days, and then under military escort, were taken to Fort Russell, and there held to await trial.

After the invaders were rescued by the military they became very abusive to citizens, which showed the true nature of the men very clearly. They felt confident that no one would hurt them while they were in the hands of the troops, and openly declared their intentions of coming back and carrying out their original intentions, which they did not hesitate to say was to kill a lot of men, the sheriff included.

The two hunters who were at the KC have been spirited out of the country by hired agents of the murderers, and are now supposed to be many thousand miles from the scene, but the prosecution has several witnesses yet. The murderers have never denied the killing of Champion and Ray, but have actually boasted of the deed.

While the murderers were held at Fort Russell they had all the freedom they desired, and would go to Cheyenne, three miles away, whenever they chose. They all waived examination and applied for a change of venue, and it is not yet decided where they will be tried.

Thus have the men who started in ten years ago as princes, been brought to suffer the consequences of their own unlawful acts. The day of the large herds in Johnson county is past, and their review is necessarily brought to a close, and the severest critic, who has been conversant with the cattle business in this country for the last ten years, will have to admit the correctness of it.

Appendix

About the time Flagg was writing his articles on the Johnson County war, the cold-blooded murder of George A. Wellman, a deputy U. S. Marshal, took place east of Buffalo, Wyoming. The story of Wellman's murder, as reported in the following articles from the *Buffalo Bulletin*, throws further light on the tense, bitter situation which tore the community apart.

May 12, 1892

Headline: "George A. Wellman shot in the Back and Instantly Killed. A suspected accomplice jailed."

Thomas Hathaway, a cowboy, who has been for several years in the employ of H. A. Blair company, known as the Hoe outfit, came into town Tuesday evening, unarmed, wild-eyed and excited, and unfolded a tale that created consternation among the people.

His story as told them is as follows:

George A. Wellman, who, since the absence of F. H. Labertaux, was in charge of the Hoe outfit, came from Gillette to the Hoe ranch on Powder river Monday evening, the ninth of May, paid off the men at work there, and on Tuesday morning, he, Hathaway started with Wellman to go to Buffalo.

Each was riding a horse, and Wellman was leading a packhorse, packed with Hathaway's bedding. When about 15 or 16 miles southeast from the Crazy Woman stage crossing, and about 10 o'clock in the morning, as they were riding side by side along the Nine Mile divide, two shots were fired in quick succession, so quick that one man could not have fired them, and George Wellman fell from his horse.

Hathaway's horse pitched him off he mounted again and followed Wellman's horse and the pack horse, turned them loose and rode as fast as he could to Buffalo to notify the sheriff.

Hathaway claimed that he was entirely unarmed and that Wellman had only a revolver on his person.

This is Hathaway's story briefly told. In the course of the day several slight differences arose out of a repetition of the story by Hathaway himself, and towards night Marshal Mitchell confined him in the county jail to await developments.

Sheriff Angus, Under-Sheriff Roles and Deputy Astell at once proceeded to the scene of the murder and Coroner Robinson with his jury started shortly after in a light wagon drawn by four good horses. Deputy Sheriff Smith with a posse of five men started later in the night to reinforce the sheriff.

The sheriff and his party returned from the scene yesterday afternoon, the coroner with the body of the murdered man a few hours later.

As the road where the murder occurred had not been lately traveled, and as the ground from recent incessant rains was very soft, it was an easy matter to find trails and measure footprints.

From what could be learned from the sheriff's party it appears that the tracks of three horses, and three horses only, were discernable. That these horse tracks led from the Hoe ranch along the road to Crazy Woman stage crossing to the point where the body of Wellman was found.

From there the tracks of all three horses lead to the right of the road about 200 to 250 yards, to the point where a riding and a pack horse had been unsaddled and unbridled. From this point the trail of these three horses lead in a half circle around and about 200 yards north of the point where the body lies, to the other side of the road into a gully or draw at this point the trail of two horses lead back in the direction of the Hoe ranch.

Footprints can here be seen of one man dismounting and walking in a straight line toward the body of Wellman, to a point within sixty yards. Here was found an empty shell, fitting a .44 calibre revolver of Winchester.

These same footprints retrace back to the draw and from there the trail of one horse leads toward Buffalo.

From Tom Smith posse, arriving later, it was learned that three other parties horseback had been near the scene. That some distance down a gulch three men had ridden, there dismounted and two men walked up to the place where the empty cartridge shell was found. At the same place were also found remnants of cigarettes, that had evidently been smoked there. Tom Smith's posse followed the horse tracks of this party some ten miles to the north of Nine Mile creek.

The Coroner's Inquest

George A. Wellman was a native of Canada, came to Johnson county in 1880, and has been working for cattlemen, principally for H. A. Blair, ever since. He was 33 years old, was married at Martha, Wisconsin, on the 21st day of April 1892. He was well known in this community and bore an excellent reputation in every respect. He was a member of Anchor Lodge No. 7, A.F.&A.M.

The deceased will be buried tomorrow the 13th inst., in the Buffalo Cemetery, his brother Masons conducting the ceremony.

One of the suspected is now in the county jail. Tom Hathaway has been in this county for some years, is a cowboy and has worked under Wellman for the last three years. He does not own any cattle himself and is not a blackballed man, nor known to be a rustler.

He has never known to be without arms prior to this occurrance and he will have some serious things to explain to the satisfaction of the authorities before he can expect to again be a free man.

(From the Buffalo Bulletin--May 26, 1892)

The matter of the murder of George A. Wellman remains as much a profound mystery at this writing, and even more so when his death was first reported.

The coroner's inquest was adjourned from the 12th to the 16th, and it appears from this testimony as well as from a letter from Under Sheriff Roles who is now working on the case, that the Reed brothers and Grigg left the Hoe ranch on the 9th in the afternoon and remained overnight at H. P. Ijams ranch on Powder River.

Grigg left the Reed brothers there on the morning of the 10th (the day of Wellman's death) and rode to his home, some thirty miles up the river. This testimony sets aside the theory that these three men were the murderers. Now, these three men and Hathaway were the only Johnson county people who knew of Wellman's presence in the county, and as the matter now stands and from a complete survey of the situation, we can advance no theory for Wellman's death.

Wellman must have been followed out of Gillette by his murderers, of that there can be no doubt. The sheriff is doing all he can to throw light on the situation. Under Sheriff Roles and deputy sheriff and Marshal Thos. G. Smith are out on the trail and have been for a number of days, endeavoring to solve the mystery.

The so-called "rustlers" of this county, upon whose shoulders the death of Wellman was instantly thrown by the stockmen's party, have all been accounted for and not one of them could have been near the scene of the crime at the time it was committed.

The manner of the killing of Wellman is not the Johnson county "rustlers" will kill, when they have to. They will kill in a square open fight, their bullets will enter in front, not from behind, when the time comes that fighting will have to be resorted to in defense of life and home.

It is earnestly to be hoped that the mystery surrounding Wellman's death may be solved and the perpetrators brought to speedy justice.

An interesting sidelight to the Wellman murder took place at the time the funeral for Wellman was held. This account of the funeral comes from "The History of St. Luke's Episcopal Church" written by the late Mrs. Charles Baker.

"When George A. Wellman was murdered May 9th, 1892, his death made history for St. Luke's church and the Masonic lodge. There was a gang called "Taylors Gang"--The Red Sashes--who hated U. S. marshalls and deputies. They found out that George Wellman who worked at the Hoe ranch had been commissioned a deputy marshall.

"They swore to kill him, which they did. There was an ugly undercurrent to prevent his funeral from being held at the Episcopal church or have the honor of a Masonic funeral. They said, 'the potter's field for him.' But they did not reckon with the courage and determination of Rev. Charles Duell or the members of Anchor Lodge No. 7 of Buffalo.

"On May 13th, 1892, the burial service for George Wellman was held in St. Luke's church. The Tiler of the lodge stood guard at the church door with his sword. Members had guns concealed under their white aprons. The minister carried arms in his vestments. There was no trouble for the gang was impressed with the courage of the few to defy the lawlessness to carry out the sacred rites of burial. The gang felt defeated.

"George Wellman's body was shipped to Bay City, Michigan. Mr. E. B. Mather, past master of the Masonic lodge, accompanied the remains."

The funeral of George Wellman was re-enacted by members of the Episcopal Men's club, at the Diamond Jubilee celebration, held July 3, 4 and 5 of last year.